The Complete Guide to

Understanding, Controlling, and Stopping Bullies & Bullying

A Complete Guide for Teachers & Parents

By Margaret R. Kohut, MSW

Certified Criminal Justice Specialist, Certified Forensic Counselor,
Certified Domestic Violence Counselor Level III,
Master Addiction Counselor, Certified Life Coach

The Complete Guide to Understanding, Controlling, and Stopping Bullies and Bullying: A Complete Guide for Teachers and Parents

ISBN 13: 978-1-60138-021-0 • ISBN 10: 1-60138-021-6

Library of Congress Cataloging-in-Publication Data
Kohut, Margaret R.
  The complete guide to understanding, controlling, and stopping bullies and bullying for teachers and parents / Margaret R. Kohut.
      p. cm.
  Includes bibliographical references and index.
  ISBN-13: 978-1-60138-021-0 (alk. paper)
  ISBN-10: 1-60138-021-6 (alk. paper)
  1. Bullying in schools--Prevention--Handbooks, manuals, etc. I. Title.
  LB3013.3.K627 2007
  371.5'8--dc22
                          2007028751

Editor: Tracie Kendziora • tkendziora@atlantic-pub.com
Cover and Interior Layout: Vickie Taylor • vtaylor@atlantic-pub.com
Proofreader: Angela Adams • aadams@atlantic-pub.com

Printed in the United States

Printed on Recycled Paper

We recently lost our beloved pet "Bear," who was not only our best and dearest friend but also the "Vice President of Sunshine" here at Atlantic Publishing. He did not receive a salary but worked tirelessly 24 hours a day to please his parents. Bear was a rescue dog that turned around and showered myself, my wife Sherri, his grandparents Jean, Bob and Nancy and every person and animal he met (maybe not rabbits) with friendship and love. He made a lot of people smile every day.

We wanted you to know that a portion of the profits of this book will be donated to The Humane Society of the United States.

–Douglas & Sherri Brown

THE HUMANE SOCIETY
OF THE UNITED STATES ©

The human-animal bond is as old as human history. We cherish our animal companions for their unconditional affection and acceptance. We feel a thrill when we glimpse wild creatures in their natural habitat or in our own backyard.

Unfortunately, the human-animal bond has at times been weakened. Humans have exploited some animal species to the point of extinction.

The Humane Society of the United States makes a difference in the lives of animals here at home and worldwide. The HSUS is dedicated to creating a world where our relationship with animals is guided by compassion. We seek a truly humane society in which animals are respected for their intrinsic value, and where the human-animal bond is strong.

Want to help animals? We have plenty of suggestions. Adopt a pet from a local shelter, join The Humane Society and be a part of our work to help companion animals and wildlife. You will be funding our educational, legislative, investigative and outreach projects in the U.S. and across the globe.

Or perhaps you'd like to make a memorial donation in honor of a pet, friend or relative? You can through our Kindred Spirits program. And if you'd like to contribute in a more structured way, our Planned Giving Office has suggestions about estate planning, annuities, and even gifts of stock that avoid capital gains taxes.

Maybe you have land that you would like to preserve as a lasting habitat for wildlife. Our Wildlife Land Trust can help you. Perhaps the land you want to share is a backyard—that's enough. Our Urban Wildlife Sanctuary Program will show you how to create a habitat for your wild neighbors.

So you see, it's easy to help animals. And The HSUS is here to help.

The Humane Society of the United States
2100 L Street NW
Washington, DC 20037
202-452-1100
www.hsus.org

Contents

Chapter 3: Waving the Red Flags................63

Chapter 4: The Silent Assault 85

Section 2: Forensic Profiles of Bullies and Their Victims..101

Chapter 5: Who Are They?..................... 103

Chapter 8: Creating Zero Tolerance for School Bullying 177

Chapter 9: Bullying and the Law..............213

Dedication

This book is dedicated to all the children who have lost their lives or their innocence in school shootings in the United States, to all the children who have committed suicide because their lives became unbearable due to school bullying, and to the friends and relatives of these children who still feel their loss.

This book is also dedicated to my beloved husband, Dr. Tristan Kohut, who always says, "Yes, you can" about my writing, and, "Don't stay up too late" about my work habits.

Finally, this book is dedicated to Eric Harris and Dylan Klebold, who brought terror and death to Columbine High School and, by their tragic actions, awakened the conscience of a nation.

Introduction

Littleton, Colorado, April 20, 1999. Teenagers Eric Harris and Dylan Klebold entered Columbine High School armed with assault weapons and homemade bombs. The boys opened fire randomly on anyone they saw. They killed 12 classmates, a teacher, injured 18 other teenagers, and then shot and killed themselves. The people of Littleton had only one question: Why?

Investigations revealed that Harris and Klebold were constantly ridiculed and bullied at school. Another student falsely reported that they brought marijuana to school; their lockers were searched, bringing more ridicule upon them. The boys were surrounded by schoolmates who doused them with ketchup and called them "faggots" while teachers merely watched. They wore the ketchup all day, unable to change clothes. In his suicide note, Eric Harris indicated that he and Dylan Klebold had been continually bullied at school and were completely isolated from other students. "It's payback time," Eric wrote.

Blacksburg, Virginia, April 16, 2007. Twenty-three-year-old Seung-Hui Cho opened fire on the students and faculty at Virginia Tech University. After shooting at least 174 rounds, he killed 32 and wounded 25, then he took his own life. He made history for being the cause of the deadliest shooting in U.S. history.

Investigations revealed that Cho was a loner at school. He was declared mentally ill in 2005 and required to seek out-patient treatment. When he was in middle school and high school he suffered bullying for his speech defects, causing him to develop selective mutism, an anxiety of speaking. Cho's suicide note showed his repressed anger toward "rich kids," "debauchery," and "deceitful charlatans."

In a video Cho sent to NBC news prior to the shootings, he declared, "You had a hundred billion chances and ways to have avoided today. But you decided to spill my blood. You forced me into a corner and gave me only one option. The decision was yours. Now you have blood on your hands that will never wash off."

Halifax, Nova Scotia, April 8, 2002. Fourteen-year-old Emmet Fralick, an outgoing, popular student, shot and killed himself. His suicide note stated that he could no longer tolerate being bullied by his peers. Investigations revealed that, on a regular basis, Emmet had been bullied by extortion, threats, and beatings from other students.

Not every case of bullying makes headline-grabbing news like these tragic incidents. However, ask any child who is a victim of bullying to explain candidly how this experience feels, and no doubt the child will describe feelings of helplessness, despair, rage, depression, and dread. These feelings have a distinct, uneasy similarity to those expressed in the suicide notes of Eric Harris, Dylan Klebold, and Emmet Fralick.

Most adults can recount stories of being "picked on" at school at one time or another. Something made them different in some way: they were too short, too tall, too smart, too dumb, too rich, too poor — the list of reasons why kids are often cruel to each other is endless. Adults can now laugh as they recount their most embarrassing school moment. One characteristic separates being picked on and being bullied: Children are picked on for a specific personal difference, usually for a limited period of time until the perpetrators grow bored with their own game, whereas bullying can continue for years with no let-up by the tormentors.

The bystanders of bullying are silent witnesses to the physical and emotional assaults upon their schoolmates. It is usually presumed that, because they watch in silence, they condone what they see. In fact, fear is what keeps them silent; fear that if they report the systematic physical and emotional battery of the victim, the bully will turn on them. They remain silent to keep from becoming targets themselves.

Perhaps the oddest result of bullying is that, to end the attacks upon themselves, a victim will aid and even encourage the bully in targeting another child. This behavior is pure self-defense, a diversion tactic; if the bully finds another, fresher victim, the original victim can breathe a sigh of relief, knowing the bully will be preoccupied by the "new toy."

The face of bullying has changed. Where once the stereotype of the mean schoolyard bully prevailed, today's bully can just as easily be female as male, since violence by teenage girls has taken a disastrous rise in the past decade. Children are not safe even in their own home; "cyber bullying" via online chat rooms and other technology is a new form of aggressive behavior that has only recently been identified and studied.

According to the award-winning weekly PBS teen series, "In the Mix," up to 25 percent of United States students are bullied each year. As many as 160,000 children stay at home from school on any given day out of the fear of being bullied. At least one out of three teenagers said they have been seriously threatened online. Sixty percent of teens say they have participated in online bullying. Researching bullies and their victims in the modern age is disheartening and alarming; emotional turmoil, physical assault, and social isolation leads all too often to severe psychological harm, suicide, and homicide by the tormented victim. Unchecked, bullies are likely to enter adulthood with perilous narcissistic and anti-social personality traits that lead to unstable, chaotic personal relationships, multiple divorces, child and spouse abuse, assaultive behavior, and violent criminal behavior.

If Americans are ever going to prevent and eliminate bullying among school-age children, there are some hard facts to be faced. Since change depends primarily upon recognition that a problem exists, adults must relinquish the myth that defending oneself from a bully builds character and that being bullied is a normal part of growing up. Aside from the suicides and homicides, being the victim of a bully is sheer psychological warfare, and many victims carry the emotional scars from these battles for the rest of their lives. It is disturbing to note that many victims share the same long-term life consequences that the bullies experience as adults. Helpless rage, bitterness, and low self-esteem are only a few examples of the price victims pay.

The case studies included in this book portray real people who were seen in mental health clinics for psychotherapy regarding a number of different issues ranging from depression, anxiety, marital and interpersonal problems, personality disorders, and substance abuse. Their names and personal information have been altered for their privacy, but the facts of each case are genuine. Cases that are fictional are clearly noted as such. Relevant information about being the victim or perpetrators of bullying covers eleven essential questions:

(1) How old were you when you began bullying others or when you became the victim of bullying?

(2) Describe the bullying that was done to you or that you did to others?

(3) Describe the person(s) who bullied you or the person you bullied?

(4) Did you tell anyone that you were being bullied? Why/Why not?

(5) What effects did bullying or being bullied have on you?

(6) Were you ever a witness or bystander when someone was being bullied? If so, what if anything did you do about it?

(7) Did you try to stop yourself from being bullied? How? Did it work?

(8) Have you had fantasies or a plan about wanting to harm the bullies?

(9) Did anyone ever intervene on your behalf? Who? What happened next?

(10) Have you ever bullied anyone? If so, who and why?

(11) Do you currently have any criminal history, domestic violence history, or substance abuse problems?

In the book's Appendix are many sample documents suggested to help students, teachers, and parents make their school a safe environment for all students. These documents can be customized to fit any school's needs.

This book's purposes are to expose bullying in all its forms among school-age children; identify characteristics of bullies, victims, and non-reporting bystanders; examine the short- and long-term consequences of bullying for the victim, the bystanders, and the bully; and provide practical, essential information for the prevention and elimination of bullying. With this purpose accomplished, the lives of many children, now and in future generations, can be free of fear.

"You don't have to behave the way you have behaved just because you always have."
— Dr. Wayne Dwyer

Section 1

The Bully, The Bullied, and the "Innocent Bystander"

Remember

03.10.2000 — Savannah, Georgia

Darrell Ingram, 19, killed two students at Beach High School while they were leaving a dance.

chapter one

Defining Bullying Behavior

"How many more children will die until we understand bullying?"
— *Parent of Columbine High School survivor*

Introduction

I f the legend is true that the Eskimos have dozens of different names for snow depending upon its characteristics, then bullying is similar to snow. There are as many definitions of bullying as there are for snow. In the end, snow is cold, wet, white, and falls from the sky. Bullying is harmful, humiliating, and victimizing behavior that causes emotional, social, and physical pain for another person.

Norwegian researcher Dr. Dan Olweus and colleagues have conducted concise and comprehensive studies of bullying behavior since the early 1970s, and his is the most commonly quoted definition:

"A person is being bullied when he or she is exposed, repeatedly and over time, to negative actions on the part of one or more other persons. Negative action is when a person intentionally inflicts injury or discomfort upon another person, through physical contact, through words, or in other ways. Note that bullying is both overt and covert" (Olweus, 1991).

It should be noted that bullying is not an isolated incident of one person's mistreatment of another person. It involves a pattern of behavior that is repeated over time against the same person(s). Bullying behavior is intentionally harmful — the bully enjoys inflicting harm, and there is a distinct power differential between the bully and the victim(s). These topics will be expanded upon later, but as an introduction, the long list of bullying behaviors includes:

- Verbal abuse and harassment

- Deliberately excluding others from a peer group

- Spreading false rumors about others

- Sending another person mean or threatening notes

- Making harassing, threatening phone calls

- Sending mean or threatening e-mails

- Actively encouraging a peer group to dislike and isolate another person

- Physical abuse

- Making continual threats to harm another person and/or the person's family

- Stealing or destroying another person's property

- Playing "pranks" on another person in front of his or her peer group

- "Visual" abuse, e.g., making obscene gestures to another person

- Drawing obscene or humiliating graffiti about another person

- Continually using humiliating racial slurs towards another person

- Touching another person and/or making sexual comments

- "Mobbing," i.e., several bullies act in concert to harm another person

- Completely and pointedly annoying another person

- Frightening another person through physical or emotional intimidation

- Forcing another person to do something he or she does not want to do

- Stalking the victim, instilling fear, rage, and helplessness into the victim's everyday life

CASE STUDY: ROBERT S.

Robert was a 24-year-old man who sought mental health treatment for his lack of self-esteem and poor interpersonal relationships. He was referred to the clinic by his mother. Robert had previous mental health diagnoses of schizo-affective disorder, major depression with psychotic features, and Asperger's Syndrome.

CASE STUDY: ROBERT S.

Robert graduated from high school, but had not pursued higher education and had never held a job. His parents were divorced, and Robert lived with his mother. He did not have a driver's license and depended on his mother for transportation. Robert's brother was serving in Iraq, and his father was prior enlisted military. Robert had no friends, had never been on a date, and spent his days watching television, walking around the neighborhood, and doing chores around the house while his mother was at work. Robert came to therapy sessions dressed entirely in black. He had some minor facial abnormalities resembling Down's syndrome or Fetal Alcohol Disorder, but he was not diagnosed with these conditions.

"If I can't make them like me, I can make them afraid of me. I asked God to help me with my problems but nothing happened. So then I asked the Devil to help me."

Robert recounted a lengthy history of being bullied at school, beginning in the fifth or sixth grade, especially by two male classmates. These boys were larger than Robert, who was rather small. The boys were popular among their peers and, as Robert said, "Everybody else did whatever these boys did because they were cool." Robert described being called names by these boys like "retard," "fag," "goofy," and "dumb-ass." Whenever they passed in the school hallway, one or both of the boys would hit him on the head with their notebooks. Robert was excluded from extracurricular activities of any kind because the two boys made it clear that he was unwelcome. Robert said that he thinks his self-esteem is so low because he was not popular in school and "everyone picked on me too much."

The two boys often followed him home from school, throwing sticks and rocks at him and calling him names. Robert only felt safe from them when he was inside his house. He told no one, not even his mother, that he was being bullied at school because he was embarrassed. He had feelings of rage and helplessness about being bullied by these two boys. He was also angry at other children in his class because they laughed when the boys "did things to me."

CASE STUDY: ROBERT S.

Robert admitted to having fantasies about hurting the two boys and also his classmates who watched, laughed, and did nothing to intervene. He denied ever having a real plan to harm anyone or ever bullying anyone himself. Robert said he began to wear all black clothing in high school like the "Goth" look and talked about worshiping the Devil; he did this because he wanted to "make people leave me alone."

By this time the two boys who had bullied him at an earlier age attended another school. He stated that a "social club" of girls began to make fun of his appearance, told classmates that he was gay, and that their club had a rule: Anyone who forgot to wear their club pin had to sit next to Robert in assembly. Robert stated that when he was home at night he would try to contact the Devil, and on two occasions he saw demons in his room. He watched movies about violence and the occult.

He discovered that when he talked about being a Satanist, the group of girls acted like they were afraid of him. Robert began to talk frequently about having magical powers and demons that would do his will. The group of girls stopped spreading rumors about him, but they advised all their classmates to stay away from him. Robert said he felt "evil" during this period in his life.

His older brother, Gary, lived with their father and was in the military. Robert stated that Gary attended the same high school as he did, and Gary was embarrassed that Robert was his brother. Gary frequently called him a "dumb click-head" in front of others, and that Gary liked to pull down Robert's gym shorts in view of his classmates and encouraged others to laugh at him.

Today, Gary is in the military, serving in Iraq. Robert said that Gary taunted and teased him in front of classmates, telling him "You're so queer, you can't be my brother." Robert said that when Gary came home from Iraq, he would like to hurt or kill Gary. He stated, "I hope he gets killed over there so I don't have to." Robert said that he hated

CASE STUDY: ROBERT S.

himself "because of the way I was treated," meaning being bullied by the two boys, the group of girls, and his brother.

Robert's story is a clear example of how bullying at school is systematic and intentional. It also demonstrates the power differential between the bully and the victim and the clearly defined patterns of bullying. While historically bullying behavior has been dismissed as teasing, childhood pranks, and being a normal part of growing up, Dr. Dan Olweus first began defining bullying behavior as deviant psychological terrorism. "The negative effects on the bullied students are so devastating and often quite long-term. It is simply a fundamental human right for a student to have a safe school environment and to be spared the repeated humiliation that comes from being bullied." (The Voice, Winter 2007).

Myths About Bullying

To understand the distinction between what bullying behavior is and what it is not, author and researcher Mary Jo McGrath debunks several myths that confuse the public, parents, and school officials concerning bullying behavior. First, the myth that "We don't have bullies in our school" is akin to intentionally denying that this behavior occurs daily in the United States and internationally.

Next, the myth that teachers and school administrators see bullying and stop it when it takes place is incorrect. Looking at the facts of the Columbine school shootings belies this myth; teachers witnessed Eric Harris and Dylan Klebold being pelted with ketchup and did not intervene. Of course, the lack of adult response to the bullying of Harris and Klebold should not be generalized to schools and teachers as a whole, but in instance after instance, teachers and administrators watched bullying behavior and did not intervene.

Another myth that McGrath emphasizes is that bullies and bullying behavior are easily identified. In reality, teachers and other adults may completely misjudge the bully because he or she is rarely a social outcast and is clever enough never to allow an adult to witness bullying behavior.

One element of bullying behavior that cannot be over-emphasized is the power differential between the bully and the victim. The bully is usually older, larger, more popular, better looking, and more socially adept than the victim. The bully's actions are tolerated by the rest of the peer group because the bully is in some way superior to them and to the victim. The stereotype of a bully being male, ugly and mean-looking, big and clumsy, ignorant and socially unskilled is again debunked by McGrath; on the contrary, the bully may be the captain of the football team, a member of the Honor Society, female, attractive, and socially outgoing. Bullies can be chameleons; pleasant, affable, and non-threatening in the company of teachers, parents, and other adults, but vicious and merciless when they turn their aggression onto the victim when no adults are present.

Cyberbullying

Today's bully is armed with technology that was unknown to bullies only a few decades ago. Technology has provided a treacherous weapon that has no limits, boundaries, or conscience. The Internet has changed the world of information technology and has made life in industrialized countries much easier. But this technology has a dark side; it is anonymous and remorseless. In the wrong hands, it is a psychological weapon of incredible destruction. Cyberbullying enables bullies to be much more efficient in their torment of others. School-age children as young as seven or eight years old have computers, cell phones, pagers, and all kinds of gadgets that were unheard of in the days of "schoolyard bullying." Today, e-mail, chat rooms, and text messaging are valuable additions to a bully's arsenal of "psy-ops" against a victim. Before the advent of this technology, a child could at least feel safe at home, away from the bully and seemingly uncaring bystanders. Now, even elementary school-age children have all kinds of techno-gadgets at their disposal to continue their bullying long after the last school bell rings.

> *"Anonymous and hard to track, the bully has free range. Because it is outside the jurisdiction of the school, the school may not pursue this type of bullying with disciplinary measures. And yet these technologies can spread gossip and rumors to thousands with a few strokes on the computer keyboard."*

Aside from the sophisticated technology, cyberbullying is no different from a victim having a face-off with the tormentor. Like other forms of bullying, the goal is the same — to hurt, frighten, and humiliate the victim either publicly or in private. Cyberbullying takes the form of written postings on Web sites and blogs, altered pictures, and viral e-mails derived from a list of e-mail addresses. The bully also sends e-mail directly to the victim with threats, extortion, and ridicule being the themes. Technological bullying is extremely prolific, much more so than its schoolyard counterpart. With a few keyboard strokes, the cyberbully can send instant e-mails to an unlimited number of recipients. Unaware that their behavior could be legally actionable for libel, cyberbullies feel invincible in their anonymity.

McGrath indicates that girls are more prone to cyberbullying than boys are, although many boy bullies do engage in this practice. For example, she describes the "three way calling attack," explained by Rosalind Wiseman in 2002: This is a nasty, treacherous way of cyberbullying because the target never knows who may be listening on the call. It works like this: Girl A gets Girl B on the phone, then conferences-in Girl C without the knowledge of Girl B. Girl A, the cyberbully, then entices Girl B, the victim, to say bad things about Girl C, who just listens quietly. Girl B then finds herself ignored and ostracized from the group and has no idea why.

Then there is the instant messaging cyberbully attack. All the bully needs is a computer. When teens (or even younger kids) get home from school, they log onto the computer to talk to their friends whom they just left ten minutes ago, a practice that never fails to mystify parents. Instant messaging allows one or more children to bombard the cyber-waves with insults about the target child. This type of bullying can be much more dangerous than it sounds. Thirteen-year-old Ryan Halligan committed suicide after being the target of an instant message exchange with another boy (the bully) who had been harassing Ryan incessantly with messages of a disturbing sexual nature.

By using the Internet, bullies are "removed" from their victims instead of confronting them personally. It is much easier to cyberbully another child as a faceless, voiceless, and nameless victim. This allows the bully to be much more vicious than he/ she may be in person. The bullying behavior can include insulting remarks, racial slurs, sexual comments, threats of harm, gossip, and rumor spreading.

Web logs, referred to as "blogs" can also be used quite proficiently for cyberbullying. Blogs are personal Web sites where children journal their thoughts and record their feelings and actions. They can gossip, complain, insult, spread lies, make sexual overtures, and anything else they choose. An entire blog can be devoted to "Why I Hate Mary's Guts," or "The Top Ten Sluts in the Seventh Grade," or "A List of all the Fags in Our Class." There is no restriction on what one can write on a blog; as long as the space is paid for, the civil laws against libel and harassment are not enforced. Blogs are not private. Anyone on the Net can read all about, "I (expletive) Cindy last night" regardless of whether it is true or not.

The establishment of Web sites like MySpace, Xanga, LiveJournal, and others, according to McGrath have allowed cyberbullying reach new heights of proliferation and viciousness. On these sites, children, mostly teenagers, can message others about any topic they wish. Nothing is off-limits. Death threats, threats of violence, racist comments, fake messages posted in the name of the bullying target, plans for suicide, even digital photos of a personal nature are found on these Web sites. Messages of this sort can be instantly forwarded to literally hundreds of other users. Cyberbullies often assume the identity of their target, and in his/her name, send messages about being gay or lesbian and having a crush on someone of the same sex. They also send death threats to other users – using the name of the target.

Technology is growing faster than our understanding of how it can be used for harm as well as for good. This leads to a lack of parental control over what children are doing on the computer. A good deal of attention is paid to sexual predators on the Internet, as well as cybertheft of identities. Yet cyberbullying is virtually unknown to parents. Children would have it remain this way so they can continue their dangerous behavior in cyberspace.

The Anti-Bullying Act of 2005 (H.R. 284), introduced in the House of Representatives, includes cyberbullying in its definition of bullying behavior if the bullying is done on school computers and other forms of technology. Schools that comply with federal guidelines to discourage bullying at school may apply for federal grants to develop anti-bullying programs and interventions.

While it is admirable that the federal government has turned the spotlight on bullying, bringing the problem out into the open with ever-increasing awareness, the great majority of cyberbullying takes place away from school property. A bully can sit down at his or her own PC at home and wreak havoc in the life of a victim within nano-seconds. Gossip, rumors, threats, humiliating lies, name-calling, altered photos, and drawings – cyberbullying of this sort has a huge audience in comparison to a mere classroom of 20 students. Home, once a harbor of safety for the victim, is now merely an extension of the battlefield.

Teasing and Bullying

Bullying behavior is either overt or covert actions. Overt actions involve direct, open attacks on the victim, while covert bullying may not be visible to others. The harshest, most damaging covert bullying consists of social isolation of the victim, being completely ignored and excluded from a peer group. Since school-age children's primary agenda is to be accepted by their peers, this isolative type of bullying is devastating.

"There were three of us, Debbie, Diane, and me. Most of the time we all socialized together, but at other times, one of us, usually

Debbie, would say to me or Diane, "Let's pal up." This meant that whoever Debbie palled up with, the other person was ignored as if she didn't exist. The outcast was ridiculed, laughed at, humiliated. The other two would pass notes to each other about the outcast. This would go on for a day or two, and then it would be over. Until the next time."

It is fair and accurate to say that just about every school-age child is teased occasionally. If they say the wrong thing, do something clumsy or silly, wear the wrong clothes, be different in any way from the peer group, children are subject to teasing. Most teasing is short-lived, non-hostile, and direct or overt. Children often tease the peers they like the most, meaning no real or lasting emotional harm. Siblings tease each other, as do best friends and boyfriend/girlfriend couples. Meant to be humorous and good-natured, teasing usually comes to an end when the subject says, "Stop it! You're hurting me!"

If appropriate limits and boundaries are not established, teasing crosses the line and becomes bullying. That line is in the eye of the beholder: the person being teased and the person who is doing the teasing. A general guideline is that if the behavior becomes mean-spirited, deliberate, and turns into a pattern of the desire to harm another person, it is no longer teasing and becomes bullying. School-age children are often poor at setting limits and boundaries on the behavior of others, even if it directly affects them. In his 1999 book *Life Strategies*, Dr. Phillip C. McGraw lists ten "life laws" that readers are encouraged to incorporate into their lives. One of these life laws is that we teach people how to treat us. Dr. McGraw writes that when we do not set limits assertively, we teach others that we can be manipulated, intimidated, and bullied. When a teased child sets no boundaries by letting the teaser know that the line between teasing and bullying has been crossed and the teased child is experiencing emotional pain, then the child is teaching a would-be bully that he or she can do or say anything with no empathy for the victim, no fear of negative consequences, and no regret about bullying the other child. From an early age, children should learn to express themselves assertively about how others are treating them.

Barbara Coloroso lists clear distinctions between teasing and bullying. When confronted, the bully says, "But I was only teasing!" Examinations of the bully's taunts clearly indicate that teasing and bullying are polar opposites.

TEASING

- The teaser and the one being teased often swap roles with each other easily.
- Is not intended to hurt or humiliate the other person.
- Sill maintains the dignity of all involved.
- Makes fun of someone in a lighthearted, clever, and benign way.
- Intended to make both parties laugh.
- Is but a small part of the activities of a peer group.
- Is innocent in motive.
- Is discontinued when the person who is being teased becomes upset with the teasing.

When teasing gets out of hand, there is a lot of apologizing going on. The teaser, who does not intend to harm a friend, backs off and respects the limits set in these interactions. The two friends are on an equal level of power and dominance. They like and respect each other and want to maintain their friendship.

TEASING

- Is based upon an imbalance of power and is one-sided.

- Is intended to harm and humiliate.

- Is cruel, demeaning, and bigoted, thinly disguised as jokes.

- Encourages laughter at the victim rather than with the friend.

- Has the goal of diminishing the self-esteem of the target.

- Induces fear in the victim about further taunting and physical harm.

- Is sinister and mean-spirited in motive.

- Continues unabated despite the victim's distress or objection to the taunting.

There is nothing friendly or funny about a bully's taunts. The victim's pleas for the bully to stop only escalate the taunts and attacks; the bully knows he or she is succeeding in the objective of hurting and humiliating the victim. "Can't you take a joke?" says the bully with perfect innocence, leaving the impression that there is something wrong with the target, not the bully. This is how the bully self-validates bullying behavior, and explains his or her actions to bystanders and adults if the bullying is discovered.

Conclusion

In the last decade, much emphasis has been placed on defining what behaviors constitute bullying. The image of a bully physically abusing a smaller, younger, or "different" child and taking his or her lunch money has been appropriately modernized to categorize a large range of behavior that defines bullying, including using today's technology to continue and even escalate the victim's feelings of anger, fear, and helplessness. In many ways, a school is merely a microcosm of what happens to a victim when school is not in session. It is impractical to suggest that bullying simply stops after school, on weekends, on holidays, and during summer break. Teachers and school administrators may see just the tip of the iceberg at school; bullying is not on a time schedule, but occurs whenever the opportunity presents itself before, during, and after the school bell rings. There is no incentive for the bully to stop his or her behavior regardless of the setting because a targeted child is always in the bully's cross-hairs.

Remember

04.24.2003 — Red Lion, Pennsylvania

James Sheets, 14, killed principal Eugene Segro of Red Lion Area Junior High School before killing himself.

chapter two

The Price of Bullying

"He gave up all forms of sport, wouldn't do his homework, and would just end up leaving school. He was angry all the time. He was picked on, period. Home was the only place he could go where he wouldn't be picked on."
— *Mother of a fourth grade student who pulled a knife on his bullies*

Introduction

When the topic of a bully's victim comes up, the tendency is to imagine a physically abused, broken-spirited child who has been systematically tortured by a more powerful, manipulative, and intimidating bully. Picture this child as an adult, and images of a depressed, socially unskilled, isolated person who trusts few, if any, others and appears to lack self-confidence. While this is a fair assessment of the victim then and now, it is considerably more involved than this. Through unchecked childhood bullying, the suffering of the victim drastically affects his or her character and emotional development to such an extent that without mental health and spiritual intervention, this is a "lost soul," forever caught in a past of rage, pain, and helplessness. As the victim grows into adulthood, he or she has little self-esteem to build upon to form a happy, healthy future. Diminished social skills, lack of self-confidence, a seething core of internal anger, and a dark depression are ever-present barriers for the victim who suffered through years of bullying. Perhaps the face of the bully changed over the years; if a child is an easy target for one bully, he or she is equally as vulnerable to other bullies over the years. This pattern often continues into the occupational setting; workplace bullying is another aspect of interpersonal exploitation that is receiving a significant amount of research; "toxic workplaces" are extremely destructive.

It is often forgotten that there are other victims of a bully's behavior: the bystanders who are silent witnesses but do not intervene, and the bully, amazingly. A society wonders why its people should care about harm done to the bystanders who did nothing to help the victim and the harm done to the bully; no one should care since they finally got what they deserved. This pattern of thinking fails to take into account that victims, bystanders, and bullies all grow up, taking their emotional turmoil along with them. Bullies do not simply stop. They eventually are stopped, usually by the criminal justice system. Bystanders carry the daily burden of knowing that someone suffered, and they let it continue.

Americans spend billions of dollars to maintain the criminal justice system, which is where a large proportion of now-adult bullies end up. Former child bullies escalate their narcissistic bids for power and control over others into assault and battery, sexual assault, domestic violence, and homicide. Taxpayers pay the bill for their legal proceedings, incarceration, and removal from society. It is interesting to note that violent offenders frequently become prison gang leaders. The bullying does not stop; it just takes on a more frightening face.

Mental health treatment is costly for insurance companies and results in missed hours of work, meaning a loss of productivity for businesses. Bystanders who were witnesses to the torment of others can experience depression and anxiety as adults. Their shame and guilt about failing to intervene in a bullying victim's distress is a keen trigger of mood disorders. Since one of the symptoms of clinical major depression is strong feelings of shame and guilt, a former bystander is a prime candidate for developing a mood illness in adulthood, along with a number of other behaviors that they view as personal failures.

Although most feel compassion for the victims of bullying, regardless of their age, it seems difficult to feel that same compassion for bystanders and bullies. However, both groups are also victims of themselves and their own acts or omissions. Society then becomes a victim – of crime, of increased taxes, lost manpower hours, and of insurance costs. Looking at bullying from this point of view, it is not necessary to feel compassion for bystanders and bullying, but it is something for which society pays, like it or not.

CASE STUDY: ANNE M.

Anne came to the mental health clinic as a referral from her primary care physician, who said that Anne, 32, has a history of physical complaints like migraine headaches, fibromyalgia, irritable bowel syndrome, and insomnia. Anne is married with three children whom she home-schools, ages 3, 5, and 8. She told the intake counselor that she home-schools her children because "schools are too violent and there's too many drugs. I'm afraid they'll get hurt."

CASE STUDY: ANNE M.

She is aware that her physician referred her to the mental health clinic because he thinks she may be suffering from depression, which may be manifesting itself as physical problems.

On the Beck Depression Inventory Anne endorsed questions that indicated the presence of moderate depression; her answers regarding shame and guilt were the most significant. A clinic psychiatrist diagnosed Anne with major depression and prescribed an anti-depressant medication along with psychotherapy. Anne did well in therapy and described many past events that contributed to her feelings of shame and guilt, including having an abortion at age 17, having a lesbian affair in her early 20s, and watching a classmate being bullied and doing nothing to intervene.

Anne said that in junior high, she was in a French class with a classmate named Lanell who was a Mennonite. Lanell wore very conservative and "old fashioned" clothing, did not use make up and perfume, and wore her hair in long braids down her back. Lanell sat two seats up from Anne; between them was a boy named Mark. Anne stated that Mark bullied Lanell in some way during every French class. She described this bullying behavior as pulling Lanell's braids, making fun of her clothes loud enough for others to hear, telling her that she was ugly and stupid, and ridiculing her religion, calling her a "Bible pounder," "Preacher girl," "Jesus' girlfriend." Mark shoved Lanell's books off her desk, poked her in the back, and kept asking her to kiss him like a "real girl." There were times, Anne stated, that Lanell would cry and ask Mark to stop, but he laughed at her and did even more "mean things" to her. Whenever Mark bullied Lanell, he would look back at Anne to see if she had noticed; Anne always laughed at Mark's bullying because she was afraid not to; she was afraid that if she did not play along with Mark, he would begin bullying her. Neither Anne nor any other classmate intervened on Lanell's behalf. Anne cited a specific incident that sparked her feelings of shame and guilt: One day Lanell excused herself to go to the bathroom, and in her absence Mark got into her purse and stole her Bible. Lanell did not immediately notice

CASE STUDY: ANNE M.

that the Bible was gone. The next day, the Bible was on Lanell's desk, covered in urine stains. Mark told Anne that he had ruined Lanell's Bible, and Anne laughed even though she was offended by what Mark had done. A few days later, Lanell was called out of the classroom, and the principal came to talk to the French class at the teacher's request. The principal talked about Lanell being bullied and how no one deserved that kind of behavior. The principal talked further about how cruel the class had been to Lanell just because she was different from them. Although the principal did not mention Mark and Anne by name, all the other students were staring at them. When the principal left and Lanell came back into the classroom, Mark poked her in the Lanell was not bullied by Mark or anyone else again. Anne told her therapist that she still thought about Lanell and felt extremely guilty that she did not stop Mark from bullying her. "I was just as bad as he was because I went along with it and even laughed while Lanell was crying." Anne stated that she would like to find Lanell and apologize to her. Unless she did this, she would be unable to forgive herself. Anne admitted that one reason she home-schools her children is that she does not want what she and Mark did to Lanell to happen to them.

The Price Paid By the Bully

Derek Randel, a former teacher and now a trainer on bullying issues, notes that, because of the power imbalance between the bully and the victim, this pattern could repeat itself later in life with other relationships, such as dating violence, racial harassment, child abuse, and spouse abuse. Bullies identified by age eight are six times more likely to be convicted of a crime by age 24 than non-bullies, according to Randel. If they are allowed to bully in school and get away with it, they will go on to be workplace bullies. Randel notes that bullies tend to have less education, a higher drop-out rate, and more unemployment. In a grim context, Randel notes his belief that bullies are at greater risk of suicide than their victims.

The stereotyped image of a bully being big, clumsy, stupid, and disliked by peers is far from factual. On the contrary, it may be superficially observed that bullies are popular and well-liked by their peers. This is an illusion, both for the child and the adult bully; they are not able to form or maintain close personal, genuine relationships. By the time bullies reach late adolescence, their popularity in the peer group begins to deteriorate; the group matures, but the bully does not. His or her school performance also declines. Aging bullies are likely to become involved with drugs and alcohol as teenagers, and develop alliances in a similar deviant peer group, including involvement in youth gangs.

In 2003, a study was conducted by Fight Crime: Invest in Kids. Nearly 60 percent of the boys who researchers classified as bullies in grades six through nine were convicted of at least one crime by the age of 24; 40 percent of them had three or more convictions by 24, the report said. In another study that spanned 35 years, researcher E. Eron followed several children from the age of eight who were identified as bullies by other children. The result of Eron's research is not surprising; he found that childhood bullies continued to bully as adults. They required more governmental aid because of their tendency to be convicted of crimes and incarcerated, they had higher rates of alcoholism requiring government-subsidized treatment, and their development of personality disorders caused them to have multiple, unstable, violent marital relationships. They spent a great deal of time in family court.

An issue that has been receiving much attention in the

past decade is whether a childhood bully is mentally ill. To some, this seems like a "cop out," a way to relieve bullies of accountability for their actions. To others, it seems like a way to explain the bully's behavior, but not excuse the bully from personal responsibility. The Diagnostic and Statistical Manual of the American Psychiatric Association, Version Four, Text Revised, contains a section on Conduct Disorder, a mental health disorder usually diagnosed in infancy, childhood, or adolescence. According to the DSM-IV-TR, Conduct Disorder is "a repetitive and persistent pattern of behavior in which the basic rights of others or major age-appropriate societal norms or rules are violated."

Four life-functioning areas are classified in the diagnosis of Conduct Disorder: aggression to people and animals including bullying, threatening, or intimidating others (emphasis ours), destruction of property, deceitfulness or theft, and serious violations of rules at home, in school, and in society as a whole. Other aspects of Conduct Disorder that may be interpreted as being related to bullying are initiating physical fights, being physically cruel to others, stealing while confronting the victim, and deliberately destroying another's property. Among mental health practitioners, there is a saying that "parents usually get the kind of kids they deserve." When discussing the etiology of Conduct Disorder, the DSM-IV-TR notes that children diagnosed with this condition tend to come from homes where there is domestic violence, substance abuse, criminality, poverty, and neglectful, uninvolved parenting. In such environments, there is little opportunity for a child to develop empathy for others and a genuine desire to form healthy interpersonal relationships; this is the perfect environment for the psychogenesis and perpetuation of bullying behavior.

When children diagnosed with Conduct Disorder reach their 18th birthdays, they no longer suffer from Conduct Disorder, but "graduate" to the Anti-Social Personality Disorder. Children below the age of legal adulthood are not diagnosed with personality disorders because, according to various psychological theories, they are not old enough to have formed personalities. Their personality and character make-up are still under construction. But on that magical day that they turn 18 they are Anti-Social Personality Disorder (ASPD) adults.

Briefly, ASPD adults have no remorse or conscience for those they harm. They are manipulative and intimidating to get their way, and they:

- Frequently engage in criminal behavior, including homicide.

- Will not conform to social rules, laws, or norms.

- Are impulsive and do not learn from their mistakes.

- Have no sense of responsibility.

- Have irritable, angry, aggressive thoughts and feelings.

- Are often involved in physical fights with no regard for their safety or the safety of others.

To date, there is no empirical, peer-reviewed research indicating that a significant number of childhood bullies have Conduct Disorder and that they all grow up to be ASPD adults. DSM-IV-TR diagnoses are sometimes tenuous; a patient either meets the full criteria for a mental health disorder or the patient does not meet the criteria. Thus, a child who bullies may have some of the features of Conduct Disorder, but the child's behavior does not meet the full diagnostic criteria for the disorder. Simply being able to imitate a quacking sound does not necessarily make one a duck.

Whether a bully suffers from Conduct Disorder does not lessen a victim's pain. For the victim, the question is not "Why?" but "Why me?"

CASE STUDY: CHARLES M.

He was born "No-name Maddox" on 12 November, 1934. His mother, Kathleen, was a teenage alcoholic and prostitute. Unwanted and unloved, his mother offered to sell him to a bartender for a pitcher of beer. His mother briefly married an older man who gave the child his last name: Manson.

Charles Milles Manson was left to virtually fend for himself in life when he was six years old. Kathleen and her brother were incarcerated for robbing a gas station. Charlie was passed around from relative to relative who did not want him. "I can still remember hearing grownups refer to me as "the little bastard." If Charlie cried about anything, his uncle called him a "sissy" and punished him by dressing him in girls' clothes and sending him to school. "I was teased and hit so much, I went into a rage and started fighting everyone. I was the fightin'est little bastard they ever saw. I was sick of being teased, laughed at, hit, kicked, not allowed to play with the other boys. All that changed me."

Because his mother could not care for him, Charlie was made a ward of the court and placed in a religious-oriented school, the Gibault Home for Boys in Indiana. Discipline was strict at Gibault; for even minor infractions Charlie, age 12, was whipped with a leather strap or wooden paddle. Charlie described his life at Gibault: "I was a small kid. I was easy pickings for those who inclined to be bullies. I saw a lot of things. I saw kids forced into homosexual acts. I was told all kinds of ways to beat the law. If you care too much about a part of your life, like me wanting to see my mom, others take

CASE STUDY: CHARLES M.

advantage of it and ridicule you constantly." Charlie ran away from Gibault, was caught, and taken to the Indiana School for Boys at Plainfield, Indiana. Charlie was constantly in trouble for rule violations. The first night he was there, he was beaten and raped repeatedly by older boys. He alleged in his biography that the administrators of the school not only knew about the constant beatings and rapes, they often encouraged such treatment for a troublemaker like Charlie. He was a victim of bullying and severe sexual assaults; in turn, he himself raped and beat younger, smaller children. At Plainfield, rapes and beatings were like a spectator sport; these incidents were always observed by the other boys and some staff members. Charlie was released from Plainfield when he turned eighteen years old.

On the nights of August 9 and 10, 1969, a total of seven people were horrifically murdered and mutilated in an affluent section of Los Angeles. Charles Manson ordered five members of his so-called "family" to commit these murders and told them exactly how to kill the victims. By the time of the Manson Murders, Charlie, at age 35, had been incarcerated most of his juvenile and adult life. He had no empathy for others. He was ruthless in his violent acts; these murders were the result of Charlie's desire to control others. Not many Americans over 40 do not recognize the name of Charles Manson; a national magazine called him "the Most Dangerous Man Alive." Now 73 years old, Charlie remains incarcerated in California. His last parole hearing was on 22 May 2007; none of the "Manson family" killers have ever been paroled; Charlie knows he will die in prison.

Charles Manson was first bullied as a small child. At Gibault, he was bullied by older boys. At Plainfield, he was repeatedly beaten and raped. These are the life experiences that, perhaps, created a killer. It should be noted, however, that at various stages of his life, Manson was the victim of bullying, the bully, and a bystander to the bullying of other boys at Plainfield. For at least 40 years, forensic behavioral experts have attempted to understand all that led up to those two nights of murder in 1969. Not all killers were bullied, and

CASE STUDY: CHARLES M.

not all bullies grow up to be killers. In all the years that have passed since the Tate-LaBianca murders that were planned by Charles Manson and carried out by members of his "family" of other outcasts and misfits, forensic examiners, including this author, have tried to discover the social "recipe" that created one of the most vicious killers of our time. Only one thing is known for certain: Manson was bullied, was a bystander to bullying, and then became a bully all before his 18th birthday. The society that created him paid a terrible price, i.e. the death of at least seven innocent people. If you create the monster, you own it.

In the conclusion to his biography of Charles Manson, Nuel Emmons, who once served time with Charlie in prison, wrote, "What made Manson what he is? The unbroken chain of horrifying abuse and neglect from early childhood on doesn't explain it all, for others with an equally unhappy past have managed to escape his fate. Ultimately, the mystery of Manson's life and the man he became is a complex one that doesn't yield easily to examination. But somewhere in this story and his own words, some of the answers may begin to emerge, allowing us to see him, and perhaps some part of ourselves, more clearly."

CASE STUDY: MARTIN M.

Martin, a military enlisted member, 22, was referred to the mental health clinic by his First Sergeant. Martin failed his "level" exams, resulting in his failure to advance to the next enlisted rank. His First Sergeant believed that Martin was a very bright young man who could be an asset to the military. After working with him for almost two years, the First Sergeant thought Martin's primary issue was his lack of self-esteem; he did not believe he could succeed in his military career and had given up on himself.

Martin was unmarried and never had a steady girlfriend. He had two friends in his workplace but did not socialize with them after work.

CASE STUDY: MARTIN M.

Martin was a young man of average height and weight, also average in appearance with good personal hygiene. He was overly formal initially with his therapist, responding to most questions with, "Ma'am," "Yes ma'am," or "Permission to speak, Ma'am?" When told to put himself at ease, Martin had difficulty doing this, but did loosen up as the intake session progressed.

Discussing the failure of his level exam, Martin said, "I have never succeeded in anything, so I guess this is more of the same, Ma'am." Martin described his family life when he was growing up as "fine," stable, no unusual problems or unique, distressing circumstances. He had been a good student in school, but did not participate in extracurricular activities. When asked about his peer group in school, Martin hesitated before finally answering, "I didn't have one." He went on to explain that he was not well-liked in junior high and high school. When asked to elaborate on this response, Martin's eyes welled with tears that he attempted to hide. The therapist asked, "Did anything bad happen to you in school, Martin?" He nodded, unable to speak. After a few moments the therapist asked, "Martin, were you ever bullied in school?" Martin nodded and said, "No one has ever asked me about this before, even though everybody in school knew it."

Slowly, Martin told the story he had never before articulated. In the sixth grade, he began to be bullied by a classmate named Tom, who was larger than Martin and was known for bullying smaller boys. Martin was unaware if any intervention was taken with Tom; all he knew was that for the whole school year, the bullying continued. Martin said that he sat directly behind Tom's chair in the classroom. When the teacher was not watching, Tom knocked Martin's books and papers off his desk, stepped hard on his feet, flipped rubber bands at his face, stole his pencils, and once ripped up Martin's homework. Martin was disciplined for failing to turn in that homework.

Tom often whispered to Martin, "You'll get yours during lunch period" and "I know where you live, so be watching for me." Sure enough, Tom followed Martin to school and demanded that Martin give him his lunch money. To prevent this, Martin began bringing his lunch to school, but

CASE STUDY: MARTIN M.

Tom took that away from him also. Tom demanded that Martin buy him cookies and candy, telling him that if he did not comply, Tom would kill his dog, which Martin loved and viewed as his only companion.

Martin never told anyone about being bullied. In the seventh grade, Martin hoped he had seen the last of Tom, yet they both ended up in the same school and in several of the same classes. The bullying continued and even escalated. Tom played football and soccer at school and was popular among his classmates. Tom told Martin to do his homework for him so he would not be expelled from the football and soccer teams. If Tom received less than a B on the homework, he again threatened to kill Martin's dog.

Tom's abuse of Martin became physical in the eighth grade. Tom frequently slapped and kicked Martin in full view of other classmates who laughed at Martin's distress. Still, Martin told no one about the bullying, saying, "Why should I have to? Everybody saw it." He did not tell his parents because he was ashamed that he did not fight back against Tom, now even larger in size and strength than Martin.

At this point, Martin stopped his story and said, "There's nothing else to say. This went on until I graduated. I had no friends. Everyone made fun of me, and no girls would even look at me. I was a coward and I hated myself for that. I still do. One time I tried to ask Tom to stop, and all I got was a black eye. It all was not so long ago." Martin did not attend his high school graduation because Tom told him he planned to set his graduation cloak on fire in front of everyone.

"I hated him, and I had fantasies about killing him, but I hated myself more." Martin admitted that he thought about suicide many times but did no harm to himself because, "I didn't even have the guts to take myself out. I remember a TV movie that was based on a real event. It was about this guy that terrorized an entire town. He was as mean as they come, and did tons of bad things to others. He even shot a guy and got away with it. Even the law was afraid of him. Then one day the town had enough. A group of men ambushed him and shot him to death. That's the kind of fantasy I had about killing Tom because I wasn't his only victim. We should have gotten together and done something."

CASE STUDY: MARTIN M.

Martin joined the military right out of high school to get away from Tom and all his classmates who had laughed at him. "I thought the military would make a man of me." Martin was an Honor Graduate from Basic Military Training and was assigned to his current base where his job performance was satisfactory, but not all he was capable of.

Martin denied any history of substance abuse problems or criminal history of any kind. When he was asked to express how he felt after being bullied for so many years, Martin began crying in earnest. He said, "I didn't even go to the prom. I've never had a girlfriend, and I'm still a virgin. Why would anyone want to date a wimp like me?

I should have done something to Tom, but that would have made it worse. You know that song by Aerosmith, "Jayne's Got a Gun," where she kills her father for raping her? That's how I feel. But I couldn't hurt anyone, I don't even know if I could return fire on an enemy so what am I doing in the military? I have all this hate and anger inside about Tom, about myself, about all those people who laughed and watched and didn't do a damn thing. Excuse my language, Ma'am. I care about my level exams, but I don't. When you've been a failure as long as I have, you get used to it. I'm just waiting for somebody else to take me on as their personal whipping boy. I know it will happen, so why even bother with level exams? I'll get kicked out, but at least I'll get away from the next guy who takes Tom's place. I don't have any past, and I don't have any future. Where was God all those years? I'll tell you; God was one of the bullies."

The Effects of Being Bullied, Then and Now

Martin's story reflects the dark impact of being bullied for a prolonged time: loss of self-esteem, social isolation, depression, thoughts of suicide, contemplation of revenge, failure to live up to academic abilities, feelings of hopelessness, anger, and being mistrustful of others. He developed a "learned helplessness," believing that there was nothing he could do – then or now to change how he thinks and feels about being bullied. For Martin, life was merely a series of failures, and he was just biding his time until his next failure.

Being constantly victimized and firmly believing that nothing can be done to stop it is a theme well known to victims of child abuse, spousal abuse, concentration camp survivors, and prisoners of war. Targets of bullying are difficult to identify because they are afraid to disclose what is happening to them; they may have been threatened by the bully's promise of retaliation if the child tells or the child does not tell out of embarrassment and shame. The child feels he or she should handle this matter without adult intervention; to do otherwise would make the child appear weak or a tattletale. This is helplessness at its worst; if the child tells, or does not tell, there will be repercussions.

MCGRATH'S LIST OF THE EFFECTS OF BEING BULLIED

- Increased illnesses, particularly stress-related illnesses
- Physical injuries resulting from being bullied
- Attempted and completed suicide
- Feelings of isolation, exclusion, and alienation
- Difficulty forming deep relationships
- Increased fear and anxiety
- Depression
- Feelings of incompetence and powerlessness
- Truancy to avoid the bully
- Increased absence from school due to stress-related illnesses
- Lower academic achievement and class participation
- Difficulty concentrating on schoolwork

McGrath also notes that victims of bullying are affected for life by their early experiences. Unlike those who experience single-event trauma such as natural disasters, victims of bullies experience chronic trauma, a series of repetitive, daily assaults upon their physical and emotional integrity. Children who experience chronic trauma are more likely, as adults, to develop addictions, compulsive behavior, depression, and anxiety. Since the child is virtually held captive by the bully, he or she is prone to developing Post-Traumatic Stress Disorder. McGrath lists the following PTSD symptoms associated with long-term trauma:

POST-TRAUMATIC STRESS SYNDROME SYMPTOMS

- Persistent sadness, suicidal thoughts, explosive, or inhibited anger.
- Re-living traumatic events or feeling detached from emotions.
- Sense of helplessness, shame, guilt, stigma, feeling different from other people.
- Attributing total power to the bully, preoccupation with thoughts of revenge.
- Social isolation, distrust of others, repeated search for a rescuer.
- Loss of a sustaining faith, sense of hopelessness and despair.

Derek Randall adds some additional insight into the harm done to bullied children.

HARM DONE TO BULLIED CHILDREN

- Lonely, unhappy, frightened feelings.
- Feeling physically unsafe at school and home.
- Believing there is something "wrong" with him or her.
- Loss of confidence.

HARM DONE TO BULLIED CHILDREN

- Death by "bullycide," a new term for suicide related to being bullied.

- A build-up of anger and aggression that leads the victim to take out his or her anger on the entire school population.

- Hypervigilence, "scanning" to be certain of safety.

For many victims of ongoing childhood bullying, the emotional effects are a life sentence. If the direct effects of the bullying are not difficult enough, research indicates that other students and even teachers tend to place blame for being bullied on the child who is being bullied.. Their lack of social skills and conflict resolution, passivity, being "geeks," having attention deficit disorder or hyperactivity that causes irritating behaviors, and being vulnerable targets results in a "blaming the victim" posture by others.

The following is a vignette transcribed from the notes of a therapist and a patient who presented to the clinic with symptoms of depression, anger, and problems with self-esteem:

NOTES OF A THERAPIST

Therapist: Do you recall your age when you were first bullied in school?

Client: Yes, it was in first or second grade, elementary school.

Therapist: Can you describe what happened to you?

Client: I was the smallest child in my class, not very athletic. It started out as being verbally made fun of like I was a "runt," and I wouldn't get picked to play games on a team because of my small size. The bullying progressed to being physically pushed around and beaten up because I was too small to defend myself from the bigger kids.

Therapist: What, if anything, did you do to respond to the bullying?

NOTES OF A THERAPIST

Client: I fought back with the only thing I could do, which was making better grades than anyone, then calling them "stupid" and stuff like that. This only led to me being bullied even more. As I grew older, I volunteered to become a member of the school safety patrol and bus monitor so I could get back at them by getting them in trouble. The vicious cycle continued because they just picked on me more.

Therapist: What was the worst thing that happened when you were in school?

Client: When I was a little kid, I had no friends. I was excluded from doing things with the other kids; I never developed a peer group to be with. I was isolated by my own choice because I didn't want to be picked on, but also my peer group didn't want me anyway. I just gave up trying. I did have some friends who were in the "geek" group. Sometimes the "cool" group singled out one of the geeks to pick on, and the rest of us geeks just let it happen; better him than us! We offered up a sacrificial lamb so they wouldn't come after the rest of us.

Therapist: How did all this make you feel?

Client: Angry, wanting revenge, sad. I think all this laid a foundation for me as an adult feeling as if I always had to prove myself.

Therapist: Did you tell anyone about the bullying?

Client: I did tell some of my teachers and my parents; they always went for solutions to put a stop to it. But it all backfired; when the teachers and my parents weren't around, the bullying just got worse.

Therapist: Did you feel like you could count on anyone for understanding, encouragement, and support?

Client: They couldn't do anything. Eventually, it would all come back on me. So I stopped telling.

Therapist: When you were being picked on, was anyone else watching?

Client: There were the kids who were doing stuff to me, and then there

NOTES OF A THERAPIST

were kids who watched, but never said or did anything. They were afraid of retaliation by the bullies.

Therapist: So, in general, how did you survive your elementary school days? How did you cope?

Client: By not being involved. I did things with the other geeks like being in the chess club, the chorus, and didn't hang out with the other kids.

Therapist: Okay, bring me up to your adult life. As an adult, have you ever been bullied by other adults?

Client: Yes.

Therapist: Can you describe what you mean?

Client: No, not in college or graduate school. Then I was commissioned into the military. The entire military rank structure is nothing but veiled bullying. Superiors bully subordinates because they can with no repercussions. They have absolute control over your career; whether you get promoted, what duties you are assigned, and how well you are perceived to perform those duties. Since other people were in control of me, I made up for it by bullying others.

Therapist: How did you do that?

Client: Once I achieved a senior rank, I could bully subordinates, so I did. I could chew people out in public, I could give my subordinates bad performance reports, I could use my rank and position to always get my way. At times, I knew I was hurting others, but didn't always care. I didn't understand how much I was hurting others, and really didn't care to know. In my world, I was either the predator or the prey. That was the way of the world; that's the only way I understood the world.

Therapist: By wielding the power of your rank and position, what do you think you were doing for yourself?

Client: I did what was done to me. This was all I knew.

Therapist: Did your own bullying behavior stop?

NOTES OF A THERAPIST

Client: Oh yes, only when I was out-bullied by my superiors at one of my assignments. My jig was up. Everyone was sick of my behavior and filed all kinds of complaints. I was relieved of most of my supervisory duties. My entire career was threatened if I didn't make some changes. My wife was also a military officer who loved and supported me, but she also knew that I did need to change the way I interacted with others. I had to re-build my "self" that was based on being bullied, and now able to bully others in return.

Therapist: How did you accomplish this?

Client: I went to therapy for three years. Nobody told me I had to go to therapy; I decided to do this on my own. I learned that I wasn't "nothing." As far as being bullied as a child, I had to let go of all that; I couldn't carry those experiences with me anymore.

Therapist: How did you learn this?

Client: I learned to notice the positive reactions of people I worked with when I didn't bully them. This became part of me, replacing my need to bully to get people to do what I wanted them to do. Even if they didn't do what I wanted them to do, that was their choice and they were entitled to make that choice, not me. I couldn't make people do what I wanted them to do. I learned to give other people what I always wanted: the power of choice.

Therapist: How do you feel about yourself today?

Client: I still carry the effects of being bullied as a child with me. I must be on constant guard against bullying others to make up for what happened to me. All this carries over into the most important relationship of my life: my marriage. There is a part of me that will always be that little kid that was beaten up, and my home is the one place where that part of me is safe. That "child" part of me still sees relationships as either the bully or the bullied; that's what relationships are. I must be able to look at that "child" within myself and tell myself that I don't have to fight or have control anymore. The "child" needs to be reassured that he is not going to be threatened or beaten up anymore.

There is another aspect of bullying that affects adults: These are people who never experienced bullying as a child, but who, as adults, experience workplace bullying. The following is a vignette contained in a therapist's session notes:

NOTES OF A THERAPIST

Client: I was always treated with love by my parents and sisters. I wasn't bullied as a child, so I had nothing to go on when I was severely bullied as an adult in my workplace. I had always been very successful in my career, well liked by my coworkers, and I received many performance awards. I was a success in every way. Then I was transferred to another company facility as the supervisor, and it was hate at first sight. Several of my subordinates took, apparently, an instant dislike to me. They went so far as to write down and keep a daily log of things I did that they didn't like. The music I listened to, my aromatherapy in my office, the fact that I was cheerful in the early morning – all was disapproved of. When I first met my supervisor, I immediately liked and trusted him. I shared with him that I was recovering from an episode of major depression and was in full, sustained remission from an addiction to painkillers (narcotics). From then on, they all set about a campaign to get rid of me. Because I had never been bullied, I didn't recognize what they were doing. Now, after therapy, I know they were mob bullying me.

Therapist: What did you do?

Client: At first, I fought back. Hard. I wasn't going to let them do this to me. I was different, and because of my difference, they were going to oust me, whatever it took. I got a lawyer and fought back. And I won. But the price of winning against them was so high, it just about wasn't worth it. I drank too much and thought about killing myself. I'm away from them now, but I still don't understand bullies. Why me? I did a good job with my work. I thought bullying was a childish thing; I didn't realize that adults did it too.

The Price Paid By the Bystander

While some bullying takes place in secret, more takes place in full view of others. Bullying is often a spectator sport, as Charles Manson discovered, even though there is no resistance by the victim, and the outcome is assured. Bullies like crowds. They like their peers to see how tough they are, how much power they have over this docile, defenseless victim. They want to publicly humiliate the victim for being a victim.

Unlike victims, bystanders have a choice: They can sit on the sidelines and laugh at the victim's helplessness and humiliation even if they do not internally approve of the bully's behavior or they can contribute to the solution simply by refusing to be part of the bystanding group. Bystanders have problems of their own; they laugh at the antics of the bully and are glad that they are not the victim. They know how capricious the bully's behavior is; the bully can turn on them for not laughing loud enough. Seeing the pain of the victim makes them want to avoid becoming targets themselves. Since silence implies consent, the bully is rewarded and reinforced by the bystanders' lack of protest. Of course, this escalates the bully's behavior, causing even more pain for the victim.

It is a mistake to think that all bystanders are just as remorseless and anti-social as the bully. Most bystanders believe that the bully's behavior is despicable, but out of safety and self-preservation – a natural human instinct – they do not intervene. "Better him than me." They do not want to be known as "snitches." Disloyalty to the socially superior bully will result in dire consequences for the bystander. They rationalize their inaction by thinking, "I didn't do it. The bully did." While this distorted view saves them from self-esteem problems at the time, later in life the bystander sees this denial for what it is: fear that the bully will make non-supportive bystanders his or her target.

LONG-TERM EFFECTS OF BYSTANDERS

- Guilt and shame for not intervening on the victim's behalf, even anonymously
- Anger towards themselves and the bully
- Difficulty forming and maintaining adult relationships based upon true empathy for others
- Desensitizing about anti-social acts, which may lead to antisocial behavior of their own
- A distorted view of personal responsibility
- An erosion of personal and societal boundaries on acceptable behavior
- Clinical depression stemming from what they see as their lack of character

The bystanders' inner misgivings about the bully's behavior are no help to the victim. The victim does not care why the bystanders failed to intervene and laughed at the bully's behavior, but sees only that the bystanders did not intervene. Not by their actions, but by their omissions, or failures to act, they are every bit as accountable for harm done to the victim.

Sometimes the bystanders clearly understand what is at stake for the victim and for their own self-esteem. What follows is transcribed from a therapist's notes.

NOTES OF A THERAPIST

Patient: El Capitan wanted me to hold this guy down while he beat the crap out of him. I didn't know him. He was some younger geek from school who everybody hated. Anyway, there was no freakin' way I was going to hold this kid down while El Capitan whipped his ass. What for? The kid didn't do nothing. He was just a geek.

NOTES OF A THERAPIST

Therapist: What happened next?

Patient: El Capitan was really pissed at me and wanted to whip my ass. I told him to bring it on. He was going to beat that kid for no reason, and I don't want any part of that funky shit. If El Capitan felt like mixing it up with somebody, he had a willing volunteer and a reason. That kid couldn't fight back, but I sure as hell could.

Barbara Coloroso notes that the rationalizations of bystanders or reasons that they fail to intervene in bullying episodes contribute to the erosion of civility in peer group interactions. When this happens, she wrote, civility is replaced by a false sense of entitlement, an intolerance of the differences of others, and the liberty to exclude some children from the peer group. This attitude will carry over into adulthood, leaving the bystander without the ability to solve problems assertively, negotiate, and communicate. In the adult world, bystanders pay the price by rarely living up to their potential and choosing convenient decisions rather than healthy and socially accepted decisions.

The Price Paid By the Parents

This is an area that, it appears, has escaped the attention of researchers on bullying. We, as a society, have focused our attention on the bully, victims of bullying, and the bystanders. Yet the parents in this triad of suffering are, in their way, victims as well. In addition to Coloroso's advice to parents who discover that their child is bullying others, it is important to consider the emotional toll of these parents.

Women who are unable to cope with a bullying child through a combination of appropriate discipline and unconditional love are likely to suffer from clinical depression.

Unsuccessful attempts to rehabilitate their bullying child are often a factor in the parents' decision to divorce.

Fathers of a bullying boy have a great deal of difficulty in distinguishing between pride in their son's "macho" behavior and disapproval of the child's aggression and cruelty.

Mothers of bullying children feel guilty and shameful of their children's behavior. More than fathers, mothers feel that if they had been a better parent, their children would not be victimizing other children. Instead of holding the child accountable for his/ her actions, mothers tend to blame themselves for the actions of the child.

Especially in smaller towns, parents are embarrassed by their bullying child's actions and believe that "the whole town is talking about us and blame us for being bad parents." Unfortunately, this may well be true. If a severe case of bullying comes to light, the gossip grapevine will be thoroughly discussing the situation and who is to blame.

CASE STUDY: THE PETERSONS

This is a vignette derived from a therapist's session notes and case files. The Petersons came to the mental health clinic for family therapy at the recommendation of school officials. Mr. Peterson is an air traffic controller and Mrs. Peterson teaches pre-school. Their children are Jayne, 16 and Brent, 14. Jayne was recently expelled for fighting with another girl and using a ball-point pen to harm the victim, a 12-year-old girl. The victim's arm required eight stitches.

Jayne: I guess I'm the reason we're here. I hurt someone, but the little bitch deserved it for talking about me behind my back. She only got suspended, but I got expelled. That's justice for you.

CASE STUDY: THE PETERSONS

Mrs. Peterson: I don't understand why Jayne did this. We are not violent people, and we have at least tried to raise our children to solve their problems by talking them through, not by violence.

Jayne: Oh really? So when Dad hits us with his belt, he's doing a great job of talking things through and not using violence?

Mrs. Peterson: I didn't say that. We're here to talk about you, not your father.

Therapist: Let me just clarify the reason for our family therapy. We're not here "because" of anyone, and we're not here to blame anyone. We are all here to help you, as a family, strengthen your relationships, communicate more effectively, and solve problems fairly. Okay?

Mr. Peterson: Listen, I work 12-hour shifts. If I'm tired from dealing with family problems, my concentration goes down. I could run two planes into each other. My job is really stressful. My wife takes medicine for depression. I hardly even see my son anymore. And now I find out my daughter has been hurting and making fun of younger kids for years. She really hurt someone this time. I'm not Father of the Year, it's true. I drink too much and yell too much.

Jayne: Poor Dad, so stressed because of "bad" Jayne. It always comes down to me. Just do what you always do and stop off at the bar with the guys after work. Remember when you got that DUI? And they still let you control air traffic. Good God.

Therapist: Mrs. Peterson, I'd like for you to calmly explain to Jayne, without blaming or accusing her, how her bullying behavior at school affects you.

Mrs. Peterson: Jayne, I can't hold my head up in town. I'm always afraid that other mothers are talking about me and think that I'm a poor parent because I can't control your behavior. I don't know, maybe I am to blame. You were always a headstrong child, but how could you hurt that little girl like that? Girls don't do that kind of thing.

Therapist: Brent, you've been very quiet. How has Jayne's behavior affected you?

CASE STUDY: THE PETERSONS

Brent: Hey, I just live there. That's all. I told Mom almost a year ago that Jayne and her so-called friends were always bugging other kids, like hitting them, making fun of them, and stuff. I told her a lot of stuff about how mean Jayne is to other kids. But it just went over her head, like she didn't want to hear it. She said, "Oh, she'll grow out of it." Well, she hasn't. At school I just pretend I don't even know her. I never talk about her. I don't talk to her in school or on the bus. I've seen her get away with really being mean, and I don't want people to think I'm like that.

Therapist: Your turn, Mr. Peterson.

Jayne: This sucks! Is this "bash Jayne day" or what?

Therapist: Jayne, you will have a chance to tell your side of the story. Pay attention to your Dad now, okay?

Mr. Peterson: I taught both my kids to defend themselves, but to walk away from a fight if they had the chance. What Jayne does isn't defending herself, it's assaulting people. I paid that little girl's medical bills. It wasn't the money; it was the humiliation of having a child who does these things. She doesn't make friends; she threatens people who don't hang out with her. Lord only knows what she's going to be like as an adult. If she doesn't get a handle on her anger, I'll be visiting her in jail.

Therapist: Jayne?

Jayne: I don't know why I do it. Those younger kids, they just bug the crap out of me. They whine, and cry and act like babies. That girl I cut, you should have heard the smack she was talking, all about my Dad's drinking and stuff. That's family business, not hers, so I let her know that. I don't know what the big deal is. I got picked on when I was a kid, everybody does. I saw this talk show once where a woman who was picked on a lot when she was a kid can't get it off her mind. The girl that picked on her the most came on the stage and said she didn't even remember the woman or remember picking on her in school. God, just get over it! Mom and Dad, well, it's not their fault. I do what I want, what I choose. I don't blame them for anything, but maybe if they talked to me more instead of yelling at me, I wouldn't have so much anger.

Conclusion

"Get tough, be a man!" "Oh, just consider the source." "Remember, sticks and stones..." "That was then, and this is now so get over it!" "Stop being such a crybaby!" These are some of the responses that children who are being bullied dread hearing if they disclose what is happening to them to trusted adults, and also when they themselves are adults. Victims who go on to become substance abusers, who perpetrate violent offenses against others, and who develop clinical depression and anxiety are reminded in an offhand manner by spouses, criminal court judges, and work supervisors that the past has no bearing on the present. Like abused children, battered spouses, and former prisoners of war, victims of bullying look and act just like everyone else.

They carry their wounds on the inside. To display their fear, anger, self-loathing, and sadness would cause them to be shunned. As long as such feelings and beliefs about themselves and their world are left to simmer in their emotional cauldrons, sooner or later there will be an explosion or an implosion. The effects of bullying do not stop when the bullying stops. A child's entire social and emotional maturity is affected by the long-term trauma of being bullied. This is a bill that is never marked "paid in full."

chapter three

Waving the Red Flags

"Yes, in fact, you are your brother's keeper"
— Rev. Billy Graham

Introduction

When (if) parents discover that their child is a bully, is the victim of a bully, or is a bystander to bullying, their first questions are invariably, "How could I have missed this? What did I do wrong as a parent? Why didn't my child talk to me about this?" While answering these questions may be important and necessary at a later time, the first item on the agenda is to take action to stop the bullying immediately and safely. When bullied children finally disclose what has been happening to them, this is their call, their desperate plea for help with a situation that they can no longer tolerate. By the time bullied children make this plea, the bullying has usually gone on so long, and has become so out of control, that if crisis intervention is not swift, the outcome could be tragic for all concerned. One has only to examine reports of attempted and completed suicides, homicides, and multiple-victim school shootings to know that, for a variety of reasons, some children who are habitually bullied with no intervention by classmates or trusted adults are ticking time bombs. With no help or escape forthcoming, these children see only one way out: Someone, either the bully or the bullied, must be removed from the equation by any means necessary.

It is crucial not to point the finger of blame at any one person when children cry because they are being bullied. Blame is neither constructive nor accurate. There is no one cause or one person who created these abysmal situations. Bullying is a societal problem, given the nature of what we call "entertainment" in the modern age; children are continually exposed to media depictions of unspeakable violence, and "action heroes" are those admirable characters who can rack up the highest body count in movies, on television, and in video games. Popular music often focuses on violence and hate. Bullying is a community problem if a city or town is permissive in its attitudes towards racism, sexism, and violence. Bullying is a school problem if the harassment of students of any kind is not quickly and safely reported and intervention swiftly made. Bullying is a family problem if children are not raised in environments of trust, support, limit-setting, non-violence, and appropriate parental vigilance. Bullying only becomes a bullied child's problem when all these social controls have failed or are non-existent.

Researcher, attorney, and author Mary Jo McGrath, in her pivotal book *School Bullying: Tools for Avoiding Harm and Liability*, takes care to debunk the long-held myths that bullies are easy to identify and that it is impossible to identify the early warning signs that children are being bullied. In fact, says McGrath, one of the reasons bullying goes undetected is that bullies take care to keep their activities carefully hidden from teachers and other adults, or that teachers fail to recognize bullies because they under-estimate the level of bullying that students are experiencing. If one knows the warning red flags that a child is being bullied, the signs are clearly present. But like everything else, if parents and teachers do not know what to look for, or what is right in front of their faces, they will not recognize it. Like other forms of abuse, children tend to hide evidence that they are being bullied and do not feel safe reporting that they are being bullied for reasons discussed elsewhere in this book.

This chapter is devoted to helping parents, teachers, sports coaches, ministers, and other adults who frequently interact with children to recognize the red flags that a child is being bullied, that a child is engaging in bullying behavior, and that a child is a bystander to bullying. If such adults are attentive and informed, and if they take quick crisis intervention action, tragedies that result in loss of life and permanent trauma need not occur.

CASE STUDY: JUAN O.

Juan sought treatment in the mental health clinic for feelings of anger that he feared he could not control. He had no immediate plans to harm himself or anyone else, and has no history of violence of any kind. He had no previous mental health history. He was referred to the clinic by his wife of 24 years after an incident where their 15-year-old daughter, Rita, was sexually assaulted by a schoolmate.

Rita's attacker, a juvenile classmate, was currently being held in secure custody awaiting action by the juvenile justice system, charged with rape. Rita is Juan and his wife's only child. Their Hispanic culture, Juan explained, made him very protective of his wife and daughter, and he was particularly angry with himself because of Rita's attack. During the intake session, the therapist learned the facts of what brought Juan to the clinic. Rita was sexually assaulted three weeks ago by a boy, age 17, in the senior class. According to the police and medical report, Steve, Rita's attacker, followed her home after school and, knowing that Juan and his wife would not be home from work for several hours, forced his way into the home where he forcibly raped

CASE STUDY: JUAN O.

Rita in her own bedroom. When Juan's wife Raphaella returned to the home, Rita was lying on her bed, nearly unconscious, bleeding from her vagina and her rectum. Raphaella called an ambulance, and Rita was taken to the ER where she was medically treated and the police were called. Rita named her attacker who was arrested within the hour. Rita told a female detective that Steve had been bullying her for the past three years.

He wanted to take her out on a date, but Rita declined because her parents did not yet allow her to date. From then on, Steve began bullying and sexually harassing Rita. He spread rumors and gossip that Rita was a "slut and a whore," that she "would screw anybody or anything," and that Rita "gave the best head in town." Steve wrote sexually explicit graffiti about Rita on blackboards and school walls. Whenever Rita had to pass closely to him, Steve shoved his hand between her legs or squeezed her breasts. He did this in full view of several male classmates who laughed and encouraged Steve to repeat this behavior and to let them do it as well, although they never did. Although they had no classes together, Steve stalked Rita in the hallways between classes and knocked her purse and books from her hands; once he lifted up her skirt when she leaned over to pick them up.

Rita told the detective that all these bullying behaviors took place in public. Her friends encouraged her to report that she was being sexually bullied, but Rita said that Steve told her that since he was older and a popular student who had several girls he dated, no one would believe her. If she told, Rita said Steve said he would "mess her up really good."

The bullying mostly consisted of verbal abuse, unwanted physical touching, threats, graffiti, gossip, and making fun of her appearance. Juan stated that sometimes Rita appeared unhappy and withdrawn, but she never disclosed the reason. Sometimes her books and papers seemed torn or soiled. Juan said Rita did not like to be left home alone if Juan and his wife went out for the evening. Rita did not have any close friends and participated in no extracurricular

CASE STUDY: JUAN O.

activities at school. Although Rita was a pretty girl, she did not seem to care much about her physical appearance. She was an average student, and Juan felt she was intelligent and could have made better grades.

After Rita was sexually assaulted, Juan stated that he often felt as if he was about to "lose it" at any moment. He had fantasies and thoughts about killing Steve, which he disclosed to his wife. He denied having any weapons in the home. Juan was also extremely angry with school officials and Rita's schoolmates; "They should have known, they should have seen," Juan said about Rita's teachers. He did not understand why the students who witnessed Rita being bullied by Steve did and said nothing about it to a teacher or the principal. Mostly, Juan said, he was angry at himself for not being more attentive to Rita's unhappiness. Looking back, Juan said, "All the signs were there that something was wrong." He said that he and his wife should have asked more questions, been more caring and supportive so Rita might have told them what was happening to her. "Now it's too late, and there's nothing anybody can do. My *mija's* life is ruined, and I let it happen."

The Bullied Child: Seeing the Red Flags

"Everyone gets bullied. But this went too far. We stood up for him, but people couldn't get the hint that this went too far."
— *A student friend of Hamed Nasith, bullycide victim*

Parents want to believe that they know everything about their children: their feelings, their achievements, their troubles and struggles, and their triumphs. If this was true, no child in our society would ever be bullied. Parents would see it immediately, and stop it on the spot.

Teachers want to believe that they know what is going on in their classroom and what happens when they are not looking —

in the cafeteria, the sports grounds, the hallways, and even on the walk to and from school. Teachers would quickly identify and stop any attempts at bullying. Again, if this was true, no school-age child would ever be bullied.

In 1993, Dan Olweus discovered in his initial research in Norway and other parts of Scandinavia that one in seven school children were being bullied. Today, 30 percent of school age children are being bullied. Based upon this truly frightening statistic, parents, teachers, and other adults must release the fantasy that bullies and bullied children are easy to spot and that interventions quickly and permanently put an end to bullying behavior.

Parents and teachers can only see what they are actively seeking to identify. To arm these responsible, trusted adults, the following is a compilation of the known signs and symptoms of a bullied child according to McGrath, Olweus, Scaglione and Scaglione, Randel and Coloroso:

SIGNS AND SYMPTOMS OF A BULLIED CHILD

- Coming home from school extremely hungry; the bully has taken the child's lunch or money for lunch.

- Rushing to the bathroom as soon as the child comes home from school; same-sex bullying often occurs in school bathrooms.

- Fears going to school where the bullying occurs; develops many excuses for not going to school to escape the bully.

- Coming home from school with missing or destroyed belongings and torn, sullied clothing.

- A pattern of not bringing schoolmates home with them; bullying causes isolation from the peer group.

- Stealing money from parents with no explanation as to why they did this; the bully extorts money from them by threats and intimidation.

SIGNS AND SYMPTOMS OF A BULLIED CHILD

- Avoiding the computer; cyberbullying is occurring on the Internet, e-mail, instant messaging, camera phones, or text messaging.

- Physical complaints such as headaches, stomachaches, insomnia, crying in their sleep, ulcers, nausea, depression, and irritability; the physical results of intense anxiety about being bullied.

- Unexplained cuts, bruises, and lacerations; the child's explanation does not seem to fit the type of injury incurred.

- Inability to focus or concentrate on schoolwork; the child is preoccupied with being bullied.

- A drop in academic performance; lack of self-confidence and obsessing about being bullied causes the child's grades to take a sharp drop.

- The child seems quiet, moody, sad, sullen, and withdraws from family interaction; the child's feelings about being bullied have taken control of his or her psyche.

- Loss of appetite, weight loss, nightmares; all signs of depression about being bullied.

- Sudden appearance of behavior problems at school or home; the child is acting-out at being bullied.

- They seem withdrawn from the school peer group and are not included in games and other social interaction; the bully has made certain that others will shun the child.

- Tries to stay close to the teacher at lunch, recess, or other class breaks; they are safe from the bully if a teacher is present.

- Have difficulty speaking in class and appear anxious and insecure; the bullying has caused intense anxiety about calling attention to themselves – they simply wish to disappear.

- Seldom or never invited to other children's home for parties and playtime; the bully has socially shunned and isolated them.

- Choosing a strange route to and from school in order to escape the bully.

SIGNS AND SYMPTOMS OF A BULLIED CHILD

- Doing things "out of character" such as stealing, lying, fits of anger, marked displays of anhedonia (lack of pleasure in usual fun activities), and using profanity; bullying leads to acting-out behavior that is a cry for attention and help.

- Does not talk about school or everyday activities; what would they say? Being bullied has made their lives unbearable.

This is a large, formidable list of warning signs. Simply reading it, parents and teachers may ask themselves, "How could I have missed all this?" There are a number of reasons why the signs are often missed, as discussed elsewhere in this book, but the most prominent reason is that parents, teachers, and other adults are unaware that these signs may indicate that a child is being bullied. Poet Maya Angelou wrote, "You did what you knew at the time. When you knew better, you did better." No adult would willingly turn their back on a bullied child. Only in the last decade have the red flags of bullied children become a focus of national attention. In the past, bullying was often considered a private, or family, problem, as illustrated by a therapist's memoir:

NOTES OF A THERAPIST

Patient: I was the youngest of three daughters. A neighborhood bully kept telling me that she was going to blow up our house. She would steal things from me and pinch me hard whenever she saw me. I didn't tell my parents, but I did tell my oldest sister.

Therapist: What happened when you told your sister?

Patient: My sister took me by the hand and walked me over to the bully's house. She told the girl that if she ever bothered me again, my sister would beat the crap out of her. That was it; no more bullying.

If only it was this easy for every child who is bullied. The signs and red flags of a bullied child appear simple and easy to spot. Perhaps they would be, if all bullied children wore these warning signs in an unmistakable manner, like a sticker on their notebooks that said, "Ask me about my bully." Children who are being bullied will go to great lengths to hide what is happening to them, as discussed elsewhere in this book. With the national spotlight on identifying and eliminating bullying, parents and teachers are encouraged to follow the truth of Maya Angelou; now that parents and teachers know better, they can do better.

The Bully: Seeing the Red Flags

No parents want to believe that their child is victimizing others, especially if they did not recognize the warning signs. It is important to remember that every school-age bully has people that love him or her. The bully is not a sadistic monster, and the bullies' parents or caretakers are not always inattentive to the child's social and emotional needs. Some are, but the same can be said of the parents of bullied children and bystanders as well. Rather than casting that first stone of blame, it is more productive to examine how the bully develops and recognize the red flags of his or her behavior.

According to Hoover and Oliver, there was a kind of mis-fire in the bully's childhood development. A "disconnect" occurs in the developing bully's ability to feel empathy for others and understanding that he or she is causing pain for others. Bullying is a form of aggression and anti-social development. Hoover and Oliver propose that aggression is a development rather than an event. They draw the timeline of this development from early childhood, which involves poor parental discipline and monitoring, which leads to early childhood conduct problems. In middle childhood, the child is rejected by "normal" peers because of his or her budding aggressive behavior and poor academic performance. From that point, into late childhood and early adolescence, the bully is born; he or she commits to a deviant and aggressive life style of exploiting others. Once developed, these patterns of behavior are extremely difficult, if not impossible, to reverse. (See the section on Conduct Disorder and Anti-Social Personality Disorder). There are bullies that appear well-liked by other classmates, but the peer group has learned by now that it is dangerous not to "like" the bully. The bully's non-verbal cues say, "Like me, accept me, or else!"

In 1938, early pioneer of psychotherapy Alfred Adler used the term "social interest" to describe an individual's ability to function in his or her social culture, to feel a sense of belonging to a community, to care about events that took place in the community, and to feel a sense of empathy for others in the community. This sense of social interest, according to Adler, begins at an early age and is cultivated as a child grows to adulthood. A lack of social interest is indicative that an individual is in a self-imposed alienation from the community with no involvement or caring about its goings-on. This inadequate social interest is the prime reason an individual commits acts of violence, manipulation, and intimidation. Thus, it could be deduced that according to Adler's theory, children who bully and grow up to be adult bullies did not develop a necessary social interest in the community and its inhabitants.

The following is a compilation of warning signs and red flags that a child is engaging in bullying behavior according to Coloroso, Olweus, Scaglione and Scaglione, Randel, and McGrath:

WARNING SIGNS A CHILD IS ENGAGING IN BULLYING BEHAVIOR

- The child's peer relations appear to be based upon an imbalance of power; a bully must dominate other children and they select vulnerable targets.

- Expression of intents to harm others that are not said in a playful or frustrated manner.

- Expression of intimidating others, shunning others, and ridiculing others.

- Obsessive interest in television, movie and video game violence and power.

- Lack of remorse for harming younger siblings and/or pets.

- Verbally taunting others in a personally offensive nature, racial, sexual, and gender slurs.

- Physically abusing others; pushing, shoving, kicking, hitting.

- Destroying or damaging the property of others.

- Having money or property that parents did not provide, making implausible excuses for where these items were obtained.

- Spreading slanderous, humiliating gossip and rumors about others.

- Impulsive, angry, defiant behavior with authority figures.

- They have a positive view of themselves and are not insecure or anxious.

- Dislike sharing playthings or other belongings with siblings or classmates.

- Have no apparent provocation for harming others physically or verbally.

- Extreme jealousy when he or she is not the center of attention; gains attention through aggressive acts towards others.

- Enjoys making others fear him or her; bullies need to look tough and in control.

WARNING SIGNS A CHILD IS ENGAGING IN BULLYING BEHAVIOR

- Appears to lack non-aggressive problem solving skills.

- Have no limits or boundaries on what is and is not socially appropriate behavior.

- Have a self-absorbed sense of entitlement and need for instant gratification.

- Refuse to accept responsibility for their actions; bullies believe the victim deserves to be bullied.

Like the warning signs and red flags of the bullied child, the list of signs regarding bullies is lengthy and explicit. Parents and teachers wonder how these signs could be missed, not fully understanding the curtain of secrecy drawn by both bullies and victims of bullying. The problem is compounded by continuing stereotypes of bullies and victims; according to McGrath, virtually every myth about bullies being easily identified by their behavior, academic performance, and appearance has been empirically proven to be false. If all society's stereotypes were true, bullies would be stopped short immediately, along with rapists, serial killers, pedophiles, and other social predators. All predators, including bullies, are able to blend in to society undetected until they eventually make that final mistake that blows their cover. If time travel to 1888 were a reality, it is interesting to ponder whether the identity of Jack the Ripper would finally become known because of today's advances in forensic technology. At the time, whoever committed the Whitechapel murders did so in complete anonymity by night, resuming his "real" identity as the sun rose. With their ability to convince others of their benevolence, school-age bullies have this in common with the most infamous serial killer of all time.

Mean Girls

Bullying by girls has reached such an epidemic in the United States that it merits a discussion of its own. Bullying by girls, against girls, has been around just as long as its male counterpart, but few modern researchers have spent a lot of time on mean girls because they do not do things that catch the headlines, like school shootings and serious assaults and batteries. In addition, girls are much more socially-oriented in middle school; their self-esteem and popularity rating are all-consuming. In her book *Not Just Chillin: The Hidden Lives of Middle-Schoolers*, author and researcher Linda Perlstein wrote that we never forget the rank order of popularity in the sixth grade or the rules of the middle-school food chain. She suggested that school-age children will prey upon anyone who appears remotely more vulnerable that they are. Boys of this age lag a little behind girls, not being as obsessed with popularity. However, the "popularity wars" among middle-school age girls have an ironic twist: While boys are trying out their manhood on competitive sports, girls are vying for popularity within their own gender. In their world, it goes without saying that the most popular girls will turn the heads (maybe) of the popular boys. Among girls, the popularity wars are internal.

CASE STUDY: MICKEY B.

The following is a portion of a therapist's notes with a client struggling with self-esteem issues.

Therapist: What is your earliest memory about worrying about your popularity among other girls?

Client: Sixth grade. My best friend Diane, who lived just two houses away, and I had always been inseparable since kindergarten. Then in the sixth grade, Diane grew closer and closer to the most popular girls

CASE STUDY: MICKEY B.

and I didn't. Diane was pretty, with long blonde hair, and she knew just how to get along with all the popular girls like Valerie, Susan, Karen, and Kay. I never understood what made them so popular. They had average looks, made decent grades, wore stylish clothes, and all that. But so did I. They just had something I didn't. They were very socially adept even at that age. And I wasn't. I wasn't good at "girl games" of popularity. I didn't know what to say or how to act. These girls knew things, or were good at things, I never would be. I guess I was more immature than they were. They had boys who liked them, but really they preferred their own company. They weren't bullies and didn't make fun of people; they just excluded others from their world.

Therapist: When Diane became one of the popular girls, what did you do?

Client: For the first and only time in my life, I made a plan to get in the popular girls' crowd. I went about it very systematically, I remember. I went where they went. I talked about the things they talked about. The very first thing I did that I recall clearly is that I went to sit at their table in the cafeteria at lunch. They didn't ignore me, but they didn't welcome me with open arms, either. I kept at my plan day after day. And it worked. I eventually became one of them in behavior but not in my heart. I still felt insecure. I remember that one of the girls, Karen, told me, "I don't know if I want you in our group or not." When we graduated to the seventh grade, Diane, Karen, and I went to the school closest to our house, and the other girls went to another school. Karen and I were marginally friendly, but not very. There was a whole new group of popular girls to contend with, and I just didn't bother. Diane went with her family to Germany for a year. When she came back in the eighth grade, she was immediately popular because of her uniqueness; not only was she still pretty, she spoke fluent German and claimed to have a German boyfriend named Klaus. How exotic can you get in the eighth grade? Diane and I just didn't renew our friendship at all. We were, by then, miles apart. They were the cheerleaders, the pep squad, the junior prom queens, things like that. I was talking with Diane once and made up a big lie about hanging out with Jenny, the most popular girl in

CASE STUDY: MICKEY B.

our class. Diane wasn't buying it. She said suspiciously, "I didn't know you knew Jenny." She was right. Jenny didn't know me from a hole in the wall, but she and Diane were best friends. One day in the seventh grade, I called Valerie, one of the popular girls in the sixth grade that I got in with. I asked if she wanted to go to a movie. She said she couldn't because she had to go to a meeting of her social club. A social club – get that one. In the seventh grade. How social can you be at twelve? But I remember my older sister being in social clubs in junior high. Not me. I didn't hang with the "A-list" girls ever again. I never even tried.

Therapist: Did you feel you belonged with the popular girls in the sixth grade?

Client: Never. Not one day. I always felt like an imposter that would eventually be discovered and get kicked back to the "B-list" where I belonged. That's why I never tried in the seventh grade. Social clubs just weren't – and still aren't – my thing.

Therapist: Have you resolved and accepted this?

Client: Yes, to the degree that I can. I'm very much a loner. I don't mind being in my own company. Many times, I prefer it that way so I don't have to expend time and anxiety trying to be someone I'm not. At my age, I don't want to change the world, and I don't want the world to change me.

Times have changed since Mickey was in the sixth grade. In her book *Odd Girl Out*, Rachael Simmons described a hidden culture of aggression among girls that she believes is of epidemic proportion, distinct, and destructive. Bullying by girls, she wrote, is not marked by the physical and verbal behavior that characterizes bullying by boys. McGrath views this type of bullying as being characterized by backbiting, exclusion, rumors, and social scheming among girls. She refers to this as "relational bullying," comprised of social exclusion, dirty looks, cold shoulders, being called a "slut" or a "ho," being set up to look stupid, rumor spreading, and public humiliation. McGrath places relational bullying by girls on a scale of severity:

MCGRATH'S SCALE OF SEVERITY OF GIRLS' RELATIONAL BULLYING

- Using negative body language or facial expressions.
- Gossiping.
- Starting/spreading rumors.
- Playing mean tricks.
- Insulting publicly.
- Ruining a reputation.
- Ignoring someone to punish or coerce them.
- Threatening to end a relationship.
- Undermining other relationships.
- Total group rejection.
- Arranging public humiliation.

Social aggression of this type does not seem to be a component of boys bullying other boys. Early research on bullying among girls indicates that social bullying may have developmental and psychosocial consequences. It hurts mainly because it undermines girls' need for social acceptance and belonging. For example, when two grown women who went to middle school together happen to meet on the street, one might say, "I was the skinny, quiet one with the long hair." This might be said in humor or jest, but subconsciously, the pain of those days of social bullying is still very much present.

It is always humorous to watch a television show that includes pictures of celebrities when they were in junior high school. The celebrities laugh at their '70s haircuts, their goofy disco clothes, their acne, and their braces. Madonna without her perfectly styled hair and sexy make-up looks just like everyone else. Somehow, we tend to assume that Johnny Depp, Brad Pitt, Angelina Jolie, and Halle Berry emerged from the womb looking as they do now. We forget that hairdressers, cosmetologists, reconstructive dentists, cosmetic surgeons, and careful camera lighting all create the image we see on the screen or in magazines. Cher, probably the undisputed queen of cosmetic surgery, looked nothing like she does today back in the '70s when a smart young man named Sonny Bono discovered that she could sing despite her awkward looks. Neither she nor other celebrities like still-beautiful Elizabeth Taylor deny their many hours and dollars in the cosmetic surgeon's office. And why should they? Their money, their image, their business.

They are not us. American girls go into middle school and beyond becoming hysterical at the mere sight of a pimple, a bad hair day, or an out of style pair of glasses. Any one of these imperfections, they know, could become the target of derision by other girls. These are "Stepford Girls," who behave as wind-up dolls to say the right things, look the right way, and act as the social expectations of the day require. To do otherwise is to paint a big bulls-eye on one's head with the caption, "Target me, I'm different." Neither boy bullies nor girl bullies tolerate difference well. In their world, being different is regarded with suspicion. Children who are non-Christian, wear ethnic clothes, speak a language other than English, and eat "weird" food could become targets for a bully.

"All people have the right to be equal, and the equal right to be different."

– Unknown

Like bullying among boys, girls' relational bullying's impact is in the eyes of the beholder – the victim. Single incidents may be dismissed as the girls' social group's disapproval of a new hair style. However, long-term bullying by girls causes as much harm among girls as it does among boys. Bystanders of girls' bullying often include boys as well as girls. The antagonist humiliates the target girl to draw boys' attention to themselves as if saying, "Look how pretty I am, how stylish I am, how popular I am compared with this geeky girl. It's about me, not her," Girls establish dominance socially, while boys establish dominance physically; perhaps a battle between testosterone and estrogen. Girl bystanders receive the clear message that if they want to be popular among the girls' social group, they had best go along with their leader's public humiliation and harassment of the chosen target.

CASE STUDY: MICKEY B. CONTINUED

Client: There is one thing that really got to me that I'll never forget.

Therapist: Can you talk about it?

Client: Sure. It was in the sixth grade. I was trying to keep my nose clean with the popular girls, and Valerie and Susan were the leaders.

There was a boy in our class named Fred. His family was poor. I don't think he had a Dad. His sister was in the fourth grade. Fred was the "class idiot." He always got bad grades and didn't have any friends. Everyone made fun of him because of his bad grades, no social skills, shoddy clothes, stuff like that. One early Saturday morning, Fred rode his bike down to a local, small grocery store. Not the big ones we have today, but a small neighborhood store. The manager was counting money in the back, and he had a loaded pistol in plain view. I guess for robbers if they came in while he was counting money, or something like that.

CASE STUDY: MICKEY B. CONTINUED

Anyway, Fred picked up the pistol out of curiosity. By sheer accident, he shot himself in the head, dying instantly. These were the 1950s, remember, and some guns didn't have safeties on them. My mother told me later, since we do business at that store, that the store manager had a nervous breakdown.

All of a sudden, everybody liked Fred. He was instantly everyone's best friend. We weren't allowed to go to the funeral, but we sent cards and flowers. The whole school had treated Fred like crap when he was alive, but now that he was dead, he was the nicest guy in the world.

With Anita, his sister, it was worse. Valerie and Susan took her under their wing and treated her like their own sister. Just a week before, they were publicly making fun of her clothes, her plain looks, and her grades, and now she was everyone's little sister. I just could not figure this out. One day Anita was the brunt of really bad treatment by the older popular girls, and the next day she was "poor, sweet Anita." That didn't last very long, of course. Fred was as forgotten in death as he had been in life. Anita's mother had her transferred to another school. With kids, everything changes in the blink of an eye.

The Bystanders: Seeing the Red Flags

"The only thing that doesn't abide by majority rule is a person's conscience."
— Harper Lee in "To Kill a Mockingbird"

In the deviant world of bullying, bystanders are "supporting cast members." A child in this environment, where bullying is not actively dealt with, is a bully, a bullying victim, or a bystander. There is no "wiggle room" for bystanders; they are either involved in the problem or the bully makes sure they become the problem by targeting them as well. Very few bystanders want to be included in being witnesses to bullying. Bystanders are involved out of fear of the bully. Although they have some degree of conscience and empathy, their slogan is, "Better him than me." Self-preservation is the most powerful human motivating force, even if that preservation comes with the price of seeing others suffer. Not only is this true of bystanders, but of soldiers, businesspersons, athletes, and many other professions where the lack of self-preservation will lead to ruin and even death.

In bullying, there are no "innocent bystanders." Their guilt comes from omissions, failures to act when they could have taken the risk and revealed the secret. Bystanders are discussed in other sections of this book, but the following is a list of the red flag behaviors of bystanders compiled by McGrath, Coloroso, Scaglione and Scaglione:

RED FLAG BEHAVIORS OF BYSTANDERS

- Having certain friends (the bully) that seem loud, aggressive, demanding, and defiant of adult authority.

- Doing things out of character such as stealing, writing derogatory graffiti about the victim at the insistence of the bully.

- Demonstrating mood changes such as anxiety and depression; this results from guilt about their non-actions and fear of the bully's constant demands.

- Trying to avoid going to school or attending extracurricular activities; this is where bullying usually occurs.

- Evades questions like, "How was school today?"

- Passivity about doing things at home that they normally object to doing; being a bystander to bullying creates feelings of helplessness.

RED FLAG BEHAVIORS OF BYSTANDERS

- Are the easiest of the bullying triumvirate to cave in and tell the whole story if appropriately encouraged by a knowledgeable, caring adult.

Conclusion

Once parents, teachers, and other responsible adults understand both the covert nature of bullying and the red flags of the bully, the bullied, and the bystander, this secret world can become a thing of the past. Bullies cannot operate with the spotlight on them and their behavior. Nor can they inflict retaliation upon the victim and the bystanders since they know they are being carefully watched. When schools implement a "zero tolerance" policy, bullies are halted swiftly, and justice is every bit as swift.

Since it is very unlikely that bullies, victims, and bystanders will voluntarily reveal their secret, detection is only possible unless they are caught in the act by an adult or if they are detected via the red flags discussed in this chapter. Vigilance by parents and teachers, along with careful attention to the warning signs, has every chance of making the school and its surroundings a bully-proof environment.

Remember
03.21.2005 — Red Lake, Minnesota
Jeff Weise, 16, killed grandfather and companion, then arrived at school where he killed a teacher, a security guard, 5 students, and finally himself, leaving a total of 10 dead.

chapter four

The Silent Assault

"What consumes your mind controls your life."
— *Aristotle*

Introduction

The Mafia calls it *"omerta,"* the rule of silence. What is observed or known is never mentioned. Breaking *omerta* in the Mafia leads to execution by loyal members. *Omerta* is a rule not limited to the Mafia or other criminal organizations. Rather, it is pervasive in every civilized country in the world, by every culture, race, and ethnicity. It is just that the Mafia gave this rule of silence its infamous name. Business secrets, legal secrets, community secrets, family secrets – all are ruled by *omerta*. "We don't talk about Uncle Ned's alcohol problem. It's a family matter." "Business terms are, by contract, covered as non-disclosure issues." "Don't admit your guilt to the district attorney." "Don't tell mom I was out all night." Whenever and wherever there is a secret, *omerta* rules.

CASE STUDY: JENNIFER J.

Fifteen-year-old Jennifer was referred to the mental health clinic because of her expulsion from school. She was observed by a teacher physically assaulting another girl in her class. The assault occurred in the

CASE STUDY: JENNIFER J.

girls' bathroom; the bystander "lookout" failed to inform Jennifer that a teacher was about to enter the bathroom.

Jennifer was observed slapping, shoving, and kicking the other girl, and also calling her "nigger, slut, bitch, and whore." Jennifer stopped when she saw the teacher and attempted to deny that she was assaulting the other girl. She was escorted to the main office by two other teachers. The school principal talked at length with the girl who was assaulted, Vanessa. She initially denied any other assaultive episodes by Jennifer, but when the school counselor and her mother came to be with her and support her, Vanessa told them that Jennifer had been bullying her for more than a year. It began when Jennifer's boyfriend asked Vanessa out on a date, which she declined. Still, Jennifer and two other girls began a pattern of bullying Vanessa, including stealing her purse three times, destroying her science project, ripping up her homework, stealing and destroying her make up, spreading rumors that Vanessa was "easy," and physically bullying such as tripping her, pushing her to the ground, slapping her, pulling out a half-dollar size patch of her hair, pinching her, kicking her, and punching her in the back of her head.

Jennifer sent out viral e-mails to most of the school with slanderous gossip that Vanessa was pregnant, that she had an STD, that she had sex with her older brother, and had a child with him. Jennifer also has a "Vanessa Blog" where she writes to her bystanders about all the harm she plans to do to Vanessa.

Vanessa stated that Jennifer threatened to set her locker on fire and have her boyfriend rape and beat her. She said that all the bullying took place in the bathroom, behind the school, in the hallways between classes, in the cafeteria, and on the athletic fields. She said that there were always at least ten bystanders, most of whom laughed at the bullying and urged Jennifer on.

When Jennifer was questioned later, she first denied everything Vanessa had said. "You can ask my peeps (peer group). I never touched the bitch." Then she was confronted with her blog material, some of her e-mails, and two statements from bystanders. She admitted to

CASE STUDY: JENNIFER J.

the bullying. The police were called, and they placed Jennifer under arrest for assault. She was transported to a secure juvenile detention facility, where she was advised by her attorney to admit to the bullying and demonstrate remorse, or else she would be transferred to adult criminal court and could face several years of incarceration.

Jennifer's written statement indicated that she hated Vanessa because Vanessa had tried to lure her boyfriend away from her. Her bullying was intended to be revenge against Vanessa. Jennifer cultivated a group of bystanders who, she thought, enjoyed watching her bully Vanessa. Jennifer took special care to bully Vanessa where no adults were present, always having a bystander on "guard duty."

She had threatened Vanessa extensively to keep her from disclosing the bullying. She threatened to set her on fire, to pour acid on her face, and to have her beaten and gang-raped. As often as she bullied Vanessa, no adult overheard or saw her. She laughingly called this "stealth revenge."

Jennifer was extremely angry with the bystander who ran when she saw the teacher coming and said, "I'll deal with her, too, as soon as I get out of here." When asked how she felt about bullying Vanessa, Jennifer said, "I don't feel anything about her except disgust. No, I don't feel sorry for her. She shouldn't have messed with my man." Jennifer further stated that bullying Vanessa made her feel "good, powerful, like I was in charge." As a result of her numerous assaults on Vanessa, Jennifer was judged delinquent and placed in a group home for violent girls.

Jennifer's and Vanessa's stories are examples of what McGrath (2007) identified as the three phases of bullying:

Phase One: Trolling — When Jennifer's life history was compiled for her juvenile court predisposition report, it indicted that Jennifer had committed minor acts of bullying in the past four years. Her intake officer confirmed that Jennifer had been looking for a vulnerable victim, an easy target who was unlikely to fight back. She tested Vanessa's limits and boundaries and found them easily breeched. Jennifer knew that Vanessa did not date her boyfriend; this was simply an excuse for bullying Vanessa. She had sought out and found her victim.

Phase Two: The Campaign Phase — In this phase, the bully escalates bullying behavior gradually. Vanessa still hoped that Jennifer's bullying would stop or that she would be able to stand up for herself. Jennifer recruited her bystanders and threatened them against "tattling" to adults about her bullying of Vanessa.

Phase Three: The Bully-Victim Relationship is now fully established — The victim sees no way out, no hope of escape. Feelings of despair and hopelessness are dominant, and each day is an endurance trial. Jennifer chose clever places to bully Vanessa: in the hallways between classes when they were crowded with other students, in the gym locker room, in bathrooms, outside the back of the school, on the athletic field, and in the cafeteria. In both crowded places and isolated places, this bully felt secure that her actions would not be detected, especially because the bystanders were keeping watch. If she had not been caught in the act, Jennifer's aggression towards Vanessa would likely have escalated even further and could have resulted in a violent explosion, causing the severe injury or death of one of the girls.

One of the many reasons that bullying goes unreported by the victim is that his or her story can rarely be proven. The bully's bystanders deny that they witnessed any kind of bullying. The bully denies ever harming the victim. Only on rare occasions, as with Vanessa, does an adult actually catch bullying occurring. In 1993, Olweus found that, to keep from being discovered, much bullying occurred on the victim's way to and from school where no adults were observing. Again, the victim cannot convincingly report what nobody else saw. Still, Olweus found that the overwhelming majority of bullying occurred on school grounds. To enforce *omerta*, Jennifer told Vanessa that if she reported the bullying, no one would believe her because no one saw it except the bystanders, who would lie for Jennifer. She assured Vanessa that if she did attempt to report the bullying, matters would become considerably worse for her.

In a crowded school, threats are not easily overheard by adults, and what looks like bullying can be explained as an accident or just roughhousing. The incidents that nobody saw and nobody heard are the bullying incidents that pass for something else. School officials, just like courts of law, tend to give credence to a story that can be *proven*, either by empirical evidence or by eye-witness reports. When the situation is a "he said, she said" condition, the verdict goes to the bully. One incident of this sort will keep the victim, and other victims of bullying, from ever reporting it.

Mark Twain once said that there are three kinds of lies: "lies, damn lies, and statistics." In 1996, Hoover and Oliver reported that, in their own sample of anonymous middle school-age children in the United States, more than 90 percent reported that they had been bullied. This astonishing statistic suggests the overwhelming degree of trauma that bullying victims endured may have caused them to become bullies as well, unless 10 percent of bullying students are perpetually bullying the entire 90 percent, which seems unlikely. To confirm or disprove this statistic, Hoover and Oliver investigated further and found that indeed, many bullied students endorsed questions that actually supported peer harassment. This raises the perplexing theory that bullying may be socially contagious behavior, an "If you can't beat 'em, join 'em" philosophy. But still the assaults are virtually silent, and *omerta* rules. No one is talking about the things they did not do or see.

In the same study, Hoover and Oliver found that in anonymous self-reports, 60 percent of students surveyed agreed that bullying *helps* students by making them tougher. They reported that this may account for the reason adults are not alarmed when they discover bullying among young people. Like the students, teachers, parents, and sports coaches may view bullying as a normal part of preparing children for the world of competitive America, where only the strong survive. Finally, Hoover and Oliver propose that another reason that students become bullies is to teach other students what kind of behavior is unacceptable to the peer group. Weakness, tattling, being a geek, dressing out of style, being overweight, or any other type of difference is "corrected" by bullying. This outlandish "pack mentality" response by 15 percent of male students demonstrates that bullies really have no idea what irrevocable harm they are causing their victim(s). This is a premise based upon faulty logic. If bullies saw themselves as doing the victim a favor by teaching them how to behave, one wonders why they go to such great lengths to keep their bullying secret. Their "benevolence" remains hidden, protected by *omerta*.

The following is a passage from a therapist's session notes with a patient who suffered from depression. The patient had recounted incidents from his past that caused him to feel shame and guilt.

NOTES OF A THERAPIST

Patient: One of the worst things I did was to bully and act mean to another kid at school. I think about him now and wonder if he remembers what I did to him and if he hates me.

Therapist: So what exactly did you do to him?

Patient: Oh, I shoved him around, pushed him down the stairs once, and took his pocket change, stuff like that. I never really hurt him. I did call him some names because he was fat.

NOTES OF A THERAPIST

Therapist: What kind of names?

Patient: Stuff like Fatso, Lard Butt, Mega-Butt, Big Mac, idiot things like that.

Therapist: Why do you think you did these things?

Patient: Well, it happened to me. Nobody thought anything about it.

Therapist: What happened to you?

Patient: There was this one guy, Jack, and his girlfriend, Tina. They used to call me a fag and a queer for no particular reason that I remember. They said my favorite book must be "Broke-Butt Mountain." Jack slapped me upside my head every time he saw me, and he saw me a lot. One time he told Tina to tear out all the pages of my math book. I got in trouble for ruining the book, and my dad made me pay for it. Then once, Jack slammed into me so hard during football practice that I blacked out for a few seconds. I saw stars. I know he did it on purpose, and he knew I knew it. He gave me hell whenever he could. I never told a soul because he and Tina were popular and nobody would believe me. You couldn't talk about those things back then. I still don't think you can. It's not "politically correct," know what I mean?

Therapist: If being bullied hurt you, emotionally and physically, then why did you do it to someone else? I'm trying to understand your past behavior that makes you feel shameful and guilty.

Patient: I know, that's okay. I don't even know why I did it. That fat kid never did anything to me. He was just fat, that was his crime. Maybe I did it because I was so angry at Jack and Tina that I took it out on somebody who was probably used to being abused because he was different, and you can't be different in school or somebody gives you shit about it. Maybe I couldn't get back at Jack because he'd whip my butt, so I just picked somebody else to punish. I don't know. I didn't feel good about it then, and I sure don't now. Thinking about it disgusts me. Just like when it happened to me, the fat kid never told anybody.

Therapist: Why do you suppose he didn't tell?

NOTES OF A THERAPIST

Patient: Are you kidding me? You just don't do that. You're supposed to suck it up. Be tough. Take it. You don't go crying to a teacher. That would just make it worse. See, in my school, that's how things worked. We had the kids' world on their own, and the kids' world when the teachers were watching. It's kind of like prison, man. Nobody sees or hears anything, and everybody gets along when the guards are watching. But when they're not, the real world comes out. And you'd better keep your mouth shut and take whatever you get dished out. Teachers can't do anything about what they don't know.

This fascinating exchange between patient and therapist confirms what Hoover, Oliver, and other researchers discovered about being bullied and bullying, as well as that secret world that is never mentioned. Dr. Duane Alexander, Director of the National Institute of Child Health and Human Development (NICHD), declared in 2001 that Bullying is a public health problem that merits attention. Barbara Coloroso opens her book *The Bully, The Bullied, and the Bystander* with a terrifying portrait of what is now referred to as "bullycide," defined as the suicide of a child who could no longer bear being bullied but still did not disclose what was happening to him or her. Coloroso, pulling no punches, indicated that her view of bullying is that bullying may be a life or death issue that we ignore at our children's peril. It can no longer be minimized and trivialized by adults, taken lightly, brushed off, or denied." She goes on to describe incidents of unspeakable pain inflicted upon children by other children – while others watched – that resulted in bullycide and homicide. In each of these cases, the "role call of the dead," not one child reported being bullied, and in most, there were numerous red flags that went unrecognized or were not acted upon. As a direct result of bullying, despairing and vengeful victims stalk the hallways of American, Canadian, and European schools with automatic weapons, knives, and explosives. Coloroso notes that these children felt as though they had no other way out of the pain inflicted upon them by their tormentors, no one to turn to for help, no way to ask for help, and thus they made a tragic final exit." From Coloroso's work, it is inferred that if children cannot attend public school, as is their legal right and obligation without being verbally abused or attacked on the way to school, in the hallways, in the bathrooms, and in the cafeterias, adults have failed these children, even unto their deaths.

That *omerta* has deadly consequences, there is no doubt. Derek Randel spent 12 years as a teacher before becoming a parent coach and national speaker about bullying. In his book *Stopping School Violence*, Randel reminds readers that bullying by children, as well as adults, has dire consequences by citing the well-known words of Pastor Martin Niemoller, a survivor of the most dangerous bully the world has ever known, Adolf Hitler:

"In Germany, they came first for the Communists, and I didn't speak up because I wasn't a Communist. Then they came for the Jews, and I didn't speak up because I wasn't a Jew. Then they came for the trade unionists, and I didn't speak up because I wasn't a trade unionist. Then they came for the Catholics, and I didn't speak up because I was a Protestant. Then they came for me, and by that time, there was no one left to speak up."
— *Anonymous*

Adults have an astonishing ability to bully other adults. Nazi Germany had to be destroyed at a terrible price, as did Stalin's regime, the Empire of Japan, and the brutal dictatorship of Saddam Hussein. The newspapers are filled with accounts of alleged victims of workplace bullying taking murderous revenge upon those who persecuted them. Even more insidious is the stranger who walks into a business establishment and simply opens fire, as occurred 20 years ago at a McDonald's in California. Randel challenges adults to consider where children learn that violence is an acceptable way to solve problems or gain acceptance, power, control over others, and self-esteem. Since bullying behavior is or becomes violent behavior, Randel lists the following early warning signs of violence, as provided by the Department of Education:

EARLY WARNING SIGNS OF VIOLENCE

- Social withdrawal, feeling isolated and alone
- Excessive feelings of rejection and depression
- Being a victim of physical and/or emotional violence
- Feelings of being picked on or persecuted
- Low interest in school
- Expressions of violence in writings and drawings
- Uncontrolled anger
- Patterns of impulsive and chronic hitting, intimidating and bullying behaviors
- History of discipline problems
- History of violent and aggressive behavior, intense anger
- Intolerance of differences and prejudicial, hate-based behavior
- Drug or alcohol use
- Affiliation with gangs
- Inappropriate access to, possession of, and use of firearms
- Serious threats of violence
- Low self-esteem
- History of abuse or neglect
- Suicidal thoughts or attempts
- Preoccupation with violent or morbid fantasies
- Cruelty to animals
- Family problems

Finally, Randel identifies imminent warning signs of violence that, without intervention by adults, may result in loss of life:

IMMINENT WARNING SIGNS OF VIOLENCE

- Serious physical fighting with peers or family members
- Severe destruction of property
- Intense rage for seemingly minor reasons
- Detailed threats of lethal violence
- Possession of firearms and other lethal weapons
- Use of firearms and other lethal weapons
- Other self-injurious behaviors or threats of suicide

CASE STUDY: THE FORENSIC BEHAVIORAL AUTOPSY OF JOHN DOE

(Note to the reader: This is a factual account of an incident that occurred on a military base in the United States. It is de-classified and available through the Freedom of Information Act. This is merely a portion of the actual record, which is quite lengthy. Much of what follows is verbatim from the official record. To maintain the privacy of family members, all identifying information has been altered or deleted.)

John Doe was an 11-year-old student at a Department of Defense public school, located at (deleted) Military Base. His father, Staff Sergeant Doe, was assigned to a (deleted) squadron, and his mother kept the home with the couple's younger child, age six. John was born with a cleft palate that had never been surgically repaired. No reason was known for this, although his father's medical benefits would have paid 100 percent of the repair. As a result of this deformity, John had difficulty eating and speaking, and had the facial deformities associated with this birth defect.

Sergeant and Mrs. Doe were referred to the Family Advocacy Program after an incident of domestic violence that occurred in their on-base home. According to the records of Security Forces, their personnel

CASE STUDY: THE FORENSIC BEHAVIORAL AUTOPSY OF JOHN DOE

were summoned to the Doe home by Mrs. Doe who alleged that Sergeant Doe had physically assaulted her by slapping her twice in the face during a verbal argument.

Mrs. Doe told the Family Advocacy Officer (FAO) that this was not the first time Sergeant Doe had struck her; she related two other occasions. She also alleged that Sergeant Doe used excessive discipline with their son, John. Mrs. Doe's statement included four incidents where Sergeant Doe whipped John with a belt hard enough to leave bruises on his back and buttocks. Sergeant Doe was read his Article 31 rights and agreed to make a statement to detaining officials without the presence of the Area Defense Counsel. Because of his statement that confirmed Mrs. Doe's allegations of family maltreatment, Sergeant Doe was arrested for assault on Mrs. Doe and John Doe. He was disciplined by his Commander through non-judicial punishment under Article 15 of the Uniform Code of Military Justice, receiving 80 days of extra duty, reduction in rank, and he was ordered to attend anger management and parenting classes with the FAO.

He completed everything required of him, and there were no further reports of family maltreatment; the FAO closed his case as resolved. The following spring, John Doe walked into his classroom with his father's service weapon and shot to death three students and the teacher. He then killed himself with a single shot to the head.

The subsequent Security Forces report, the medical autopsy report, and the mental health forensic behavioral report indicated the following facts: John Doe had been the subject of intense bullying by five male and two female members of his class due to his facial deformity. The bullying began when John entered school in the first grade at age six. Although school officials and pediatricians urgently recommended that John's cleft palate be repaired, it was never done. According to Mrs. Doe, Sergeant Doe (rank restored) did not believe John was his child, and he refused to use his military medical benefits to "fix another guy's kid. Let that son of a bitch pay for it." DNA evidence at autopsy confirmed that John was indeed Sergeant Doe's biological child.

CASE STUDY: THE FORENSIC BEHAVIORAL AUTOPSY OF JOHN DOE

Information gained from John's classmates indicated that John was constantly bullied by several students for a number of years. The bullying children called him "rabbit face," "beast," "retard," ugly-butt," and many other derogatory names because of his deformity. He was also physically bullied: His belongings were stolen or destroyed, he was slapped, kicked, and tripped. The girls involved told him he had "cooties" and was "gross." They refused to sit next to him in class and told him that he smelled bad. John was an average student in school, but attended special speech therapy. Again, his classmates made fun of his speech delay, a result of his cleft palate. When John was nine, one of his teachers made a report of child neglect to the FAO regarding Sergeant Doe's refusal to have John's cleft palate repaired; she had reported this to Sergeant and Mrs. Doe on three occasions. The teacher was aware that John was being "teased" by other students because of his deformity. Evaluation by the FAO and the Staff Judge Advocate's office, as well as the local child protective service, resulted in findings that Sergeant Doe was not in violation of the Uniform Code of Military Justice or of any state or local laws by not repairing John's cleft palate since this condition was not life threatening.

The FAO and the Staff Judge Advocate (attorney for the government) were compelled to dismiss the complaint, but Sergeant Doe was disciplined by his Commander with a Letter of Reprimand for "reckless disregard for his child's welfare." This LOR and the previous year's Article 15 action would prevent Sergeant Doe from re-enlisting, and he would be administratively separated from service. After the school shooting, a search by Security Forces and the Mental Health Flight Commander of John's room revealed three notebooks of drawings that represented graphic violence against boys and girls. The pictures were of dead bodies that had been shot, knifed, and hung. One of the boys bore a resemblance to John himself.

There were several drawings of an adult male who had been literally hacked into pieces. Also found in John's room was the holster of his

CASE STUDY: THE FORENSIC BEHAVIORAL AUTOPSY OF JOHN DOE

father's service weapon and 20 rounds of ammunition. Sergeant Doe was arrested on the spot for failure to secure his service weapon and detained in correctional custody. His Commander declined to sign for his release.

John's room contained 17 DVD movies, all of a graphically violent nature. Further investigation of the crime scene identified the three dead students as among those who had been bullying John since age six – two of the boys and one of the girls. John's motive for killing his teacher remains unknown, but forensic investigators determined that the teacher was moving towards John when she was killed; John may have panicked and killed her without intent.

A search of John's body revealed 40 rounds of ammunition, indicating that he may have planned to kill many more people that day. In concluding reports, it was determined that he had been a victim of bullying for six years because of his deformity.

He told no one about being bullied, having been repeatedly threatened with even more maltreatment if he reported the incidents. Before his death, according to Mrs. Doe, John seemed angry, withdrawn, had numerous physical complaints requiring trips to his pediatrician, and was preoccupied with violence on television and in movies that he watched against his parents' rules. The deaths of the three students and the teacher were ruled as homicides, and John's death was ruled as suicide.

Conclusion

Bullying is a silent assault for a variety of reasons that have been discussed. Its consequences are agonizing and at times even deadly. Increasing incidents of bullycide and homicide by children clearly indicate that these silent assaults upon the world's children result in desperate acts of escape from their tormentors and are red flags that, unless adults intervene, they are failing these children. Adults who are bullied have options; children do not.

"If you care too much about what other people think of you, you will always be their prisoner."

(Lao Tzu)

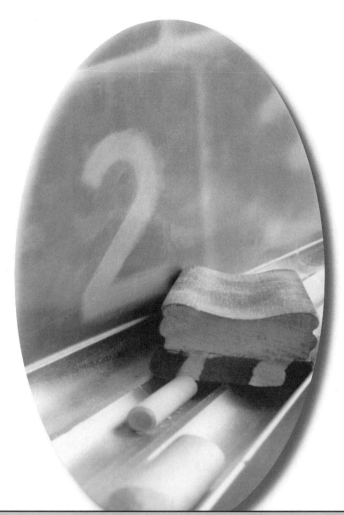

Remember

12.06.1999 — Fort Gibson, Oklahoma

Seth Trickey, 13, opened fire with a 9mm semiautomatic handgun at Fort Gibson Middle School, wounding four students.

Section 2

Forensic Profiles of Bullies
and Their Victims

Remember

01.03.2007 — Tacoma, Washington

Douglas Chanthabouly, 18, shot fellow student Samnang Kok, 17, in the hallway of Henry Foss High School.

chapter five

Who Are They?

Introduction

How easy it would be if those who mean us harm wore a sign around their necks saying, "Don't come near me; I will hurt you. Don't ever trust me; I will betray you." In this idyllic society, there would be no murder, no rape, no assault, no domestic violence – and no bullying. Workplaces, homes, and schools would be safe places. Our prisons would hold only those who committed non-violent offenses. There would be no more death penalty. We would be able to feel safe when we walk the streets, go to school, or enter our homes. Hitler, Stalin, Saddam Hussein, and Osama bin Laden would never have existed. John Gacy, who raped and murdered 33 young men and boys, would never have existed. The Columbine school shootings would never have happened.

Since this world exists only in our fantasies and dreams, we must cope with the world as we know it. In our world, thousands of innocent men and women were killed on 11 September 2001. Each day, children are abducted, sexually assaulted, and killed by vicious, faceless pedophiles who, for the most part, are never apprehended. Each day, thousands of children are bullied at school by psychological and physical violence. Bullying is so under-reported that few adults know it is occurring until the school violence and suicides make headlines. Why did we not know? True, bullies, victims of bullying, and bystanders to bullying are not wearing signs that identify them. Nevertheless, there are behavioral signs that, if we take the time to look, are always present when our schoolchildren are in danger or who are causing danger for others. Some of these signs were discussed in the previous chapter as "red flags" that a child was being bullied. This chapter delves more deeply, past the "red flags," into forensic characteristics of the bully, the victim, and the bystanders.

On March 5, 2001, in Santee, California, Charles Andrew Williams, a 15-year-old high school freshman, shot and killed two classmates. He wounded 13 other classmates, as well as several adults. Why? He was bullied continuously. His "crime?" He was very thin and had big ears. Charles told his older brother that he was called "Anorexic Andy." A witness to the shooting stated, "We abused him pretty much. I mean verbally. I called him a skinny faggot one time." Investigators found that the bullying went much farther than name-calling. Andy was burned on the neck with a cigarette lighter, had his head dunked in a toilet containing urine and feces, was punched in the face, and was subjected to an unsuccessful attempt to set him on fire. Andy warned at least 12 people that he was going to "do a Columbine." He was tried as an adult and sentenced to 50 years to life for his actions. Those that bullied Andy were unpunished.

These questions remain unanswered: Why was Andy never considered as a possible bullying victim? Why did the peers he warned not report his threats? Why did bystanders not only fail to report the bullying, but in some cases, joined the bully/bullies in taunting Andy? Why was the bully/bullies not identified much earlier? Perhaps, through early intervention and by gaining important information about the profiles of bullies, their victims, and bystanders, a significant number of suicides and homicides may not occur.

The use of the term "forensic" in this chapter refers to an analysis of behavior that does not fall within social norms, creates significant personal distress, and may be illegal.

The Forensic Profile of a Bully

A bully is not born; he or she is "made." No one factor in a bully's social or family environment tells the complete story. Bullying is learned behavior. Barbara Coloroso (2003) describes seven kinds of bullies (gender neutral):

THE SEVEN KINDS OF BULLIES	
The Confident Bully	Has a big ego, but not a strong one, an inflated sense of self, a sense of entitlement, a liking for violence, and has no empathy for those he hurts. This bully only feels important when inflicting pain upon others. He has a powerful, overwhelming personality and feels superior to others.
The Social Bully	Prefers rumor, gossip, verbal taunts and shunning, isolating the victim, and excluding her from school activities. She has a poor sense of self and hides her insecurities in a cloak of charm and exaggerated confidence.
The Fully Armored Bully	Comes across to others as being cool and detached. He shows little emotion. He looks for opportunities to bully when he cannot be seen and caught. He is cruel and vicious to his target but charming in front of others.

THE SEVEN KINDS OF BULLIES	
The Hyperactive Bully	Struggles with his schoolwork and has poor social skills because he does not process social cues accurately; he perceives that others want to harm him and reacts aggressively to these non-existent cues. "I'll get them before they get me."
The Bunch of Bullies	A group of friends who, together, do things that they would not do if alone. Their goal is to isolate, exclude, and scapegoat their target.
The Gang of Bullies	Forms not out of friendship but as a strategic alliance that pursues power, control, domination, and subjugation over others. Drawn together, they bully others to gain respect from their gang, and lack empathy and remorse for their actions.
The Bullied Bully	Is both a target and a bully. She is bullied by older kids and by adults; she bullies others of her same-age or younger peer group to feel relief from her sense of powerlessness and self-hatred.

According to Coloroso, even though their ways of bullying and their personality styles are different, bullies have several characteristics in common:

COMMON BULLY CHARACTERISTICS
• They like to dominate others.
• They use others to get what they want.
• They have difficulty seeing a situation from another's vantage point.
• Their feelings and needs take priority over others' needs and rights.
• They hurt other children when adults are not present.
• They use blame and false allegations to project their own low self-worth onto their victim(s).

COMMON BULLY CHARACTERISTICS

- They don't accept responsibility for their actions.
- They cannot foresee the consequences of their actions.
- They crave attention.
- They feel contempt towards their victims as being worthless, inferior, and not worthy of respect.

In their profile of a bully, Scaglione and Scaglione (2006) describe a "pure" bully as one who is driven by the need to be respected and popular. Having a strong sense of entitlement and empowerment, these bullies pursue power and control over others; they have the power to make their victim feel sad and humiliated. This behavior is possibly learned from their home environment.

Pure bullies rationalize their actions by telling themselves and others that the victim(s) deserves to be bullied. It is fun and humorous to cause pain to another person. They are just "having a little fun." It does not bother them that their "fun" is gained at the expense of another person.

Scaglione and Scaglione (2006) disagree with Coloroso and others who believe that bullies have low self-esteem and that they bully because they do not think well of themselves. They write that most experts see just the opposite. The bully is a popular student with high self-esteem who wants respect from peers. By pursuing others to make fun of, they feel they will earn the respect of their peers. The unfortunate thing is that in many cases, they do.

In his profile of a bully, Randel emphasizes that since bullying is learned behavior, he or she is likely to live in an unstable home environment. Anger, Randel wrote, is the overwhelming emotion of a bully: anger due to poverty, the lack of strong parental figures, domestic violence in the home, alcohol and drug abuse by parents, his/her learning disabilities, the death or incarceration of a parent, and anger about the feeling that he/she is unwanted, disregarded, and unloved at home. Randel speculates that bullies learn their behavior because their parents are over-punitive, non-attentive, rigid, authoritarian, and/or abusive. In their early home interactions, they see that violent, aggressive behavior is rewarded by the gain of power over another person. The would-be bully's parents foster a lack of bonding, and do not establish limits and boundaries upon behavior for themselves or their children.

CASE STUDY: DEVIN T.

Devin is a 13-year-old African American boy who was expelled from public school, where he was an eighth grade student. He made poor to average grades in school and stated that he did not really apply himself in school because it was unimportant to him. Since his expulsion, Devin's mother has been trying to enroll him in a private group home and school for troubled boys.

One of the conditions of his enrollment in this program is a clinical behavioral and emotional evaluation. Devin was expelled from school because a teacher observed him slapping a younger, smaller boy repeatedly and demanding that the boy give him all his pocket money. This is the fifth time Devin has been caught by an adult bullying a younger boy. Each time, Devin's mother was called to the school and Devin was suspended for up to a week. Devin's mother did not follow through with suggestions by the school counselor to set firm limits on Devin's behavior. Devin does not know who his natural father is; he describes his mother as a "dumb whore drug addict who doesn't even know I'm there." He and his mother live in a housing project with Devin's two younger siblings. Since his mother is unemployed, the family lives on public assistance. Devin has no known gang affiliation. He is generally

CASE STUDY: DEVIN T.

well-liked by his "peeps" (peers) but has no really close friendships.

Devin admits that he bullies younger, smaller boys. This behavior began when he was nine years old. He stated, "It made me feel good that kids had to do what I say." Devin denies that he has been abused in any way by family members or his peer group. He has no known substance abuse problems, but describes his mother as a "crack whore." "She just ain't there. Never has been. I make my own rules." Devin admits that he has experimented with alcohol, marijuana, crack cocaine, and methamphetamine. He does not think he is addicted to these substances, but used them, "to make everything go away."

When asked to describe how he bullied others, Devin stated," If they have something I want, like a cool pair of shoes, I take it. If they have money, I take that, too. If they're goofy or dumb, I just slap 'em around, punch 'em in the stomach, trip them, or jerk their hair really hard. Some dumb-ass nigger that don't do what I say is gonna get his ass whupped." Devin avoids bystanders when he bullies another child because, "…I don't want no witnesses. I can deny it. Nobody's gonna believe some whiny cry-baby." When asked about the consequences of his actions, Devin stated, "Man, I don't care. So what if they send me to that group place. It's better than what I got right now. If I don't like it I'll just split."

Devin discussed his feelings about bullying others. "I don't give a damn what they feel about it. They got it coming. I'd show them respect if they fought back, but if they're just gonna stand there and get whupped, I'll hit 'em even harder.

I don't "carry" (weapons) because I don't need to. I let my hands do the talking. But if some dude wants to throw down with me, I'd kill him in a heartbeat."

Based upon other aspects of this interview, Devin was diagnosed with Conduct Disorder. He was taken into the state's custody and sent to the group home. His mother visited him only one time; she was observed giving Devin a vial of "rush," an inhalant. She was arrested and her parental rights were

CASE STUDY: DEVIN T.

terminated. Devin did fairly well at the group home; he obeyed limits and boundaries set upon his behavior, and, as far as the staff knew, did not attempt to bully other residents; most were larger than Devin and had committed crimes that resulted in their placement at the group home. Devin found no easy targets, and kept to himself as much as he could.

Since bullying is a learned anti-social behavior, the first step in any intervention with these school-age children is to discover who modeled this behavior for them: parents, siblings, peers, or media violence. None of these modeling examples are mutually exclusive; the bully may learn his or her behavior from all these sources. Devin has the final word on this subject:

"This is just how things are, man. Not just me. Lots of kids. I've heard all that talk about some kids being a "bad seed." I guess that means we were born this way, and we'll never change, so what the (expletive). See, everything is divided as cool or un-cool. If everything is cool, you don't got to worry about anything. But if everything is un-cool, you better watch your back because when you get out on the street, you've gotta be cool or nothing good will ever happen."

The Forensic Profile of a Victim

Aside from actually being one, it can be difficult to determine if a child is being bullied. As described earlier, the rule of *omerta* protects the bully's anonymity, especially when the victim either denies being a victim, or declines, for safety reasons, to identify the bully. It is embarrassing for kids to tell an adult that he or she is being bullied. A victim views this as admitting to weakness, fear, and vulnerability. It seems much easier to wait it out and endure the bullying until they leave school. This strategy, however, is potentially dangerous for the victim in two ways:

(1) Being bullied as a child may predict that the victim will become victimized again in the workplace. Nothing changes for the victim except the scenery and the individuals involved. Workplace bullying is just as vicious as school bullying and can have tragic results, i.e. suicides and homicides.

(2) The school-age victim is unlikely to have the assertive skills to end or endure the bullying. Just within the past decade, research has indicated that victims either grow up with abysmal, dysfunctional self-images, but they are also capable of "snapping" when they can endure no more. The Columbine school shootings were well-planned in advance; other fatal reactions to bullying at school have been impulsive.

In 1993, Olweus identified some general characteristics of a bullied child:

GENERAL CHARACTERISTICS OF A BULLIED CHILD

- May be physically weaker than their peers.
- May have "body anxiety" and are afraid of getting hurt. Physically ineffective in playing games, sports, and have poor coordination.
- Are cautious, sensitive, quiet, withdrawn, passive, submissive, and shy. Cries easily.
- Are anxious, insecure, and have a negative view of him or herself.
- Have difficulty being assertive in the peer group.

GENERAL CHARACTERISTICS OF A BULLIED CHILD

- Often relate better to adults than to peers.
- May be hyperactive, clumsy, have irritating habits or mannerisms.
- May be physically unattractive, e.g. overweight, underweight, have severe acne, are short in stature, and have poor personal grooming.

Unknowingly, Olweus explained, these children send out "signals" that they are worthless and inadequate and will not retaliate if they are bullied. They become "easy targets."

Randel, drawing upon his years of teaching, observed that some victims of bullying may be very intelligent and enjoy school. For this, he or she may be called derogatory names; it is even worse for them if they cry. Once labeled a "cry baby smart ass," that label tends to stick with them for years to come.

"I learned long ago, never wrestle with a pig. You get dirty, and the pig loves it."
– Cyrus Ching

Bullies know who will and will not fight back. They never put themselves in a situation where they might come out as the loser. They must be physically and socially superior to their victim. This they enjoy, and they take pride in the fact that they can physically overpower the victim. Very few victims even try to defend themselves. This passivity, too, is learned behavior just as bullying is. Victims learn not to fight back since they know they have no chance of winning. Bullies learn early never to corner someone who is meaner than they are.

A child can be victimized because of his/her race, religion, cultural customs, or native language. Racial and religious stereotypes have existed for hundreds of years. Although this may not be bullying in its purest form, it teaches children that they are different in some way; sometimes differences are not tolerated. Modern-day prophets, including poets, artists, writers, musicians, and screen actors/actresses decry hate and intolerance. Rock and roll megastar, Ozzy Osbourne, who created the genre of music known as "heavy metal," often steps down from his performance persona as the "Prince of Darkness" to speak from his heart to listeners everywhere:

"I wish we all could only find serenity;
It would be nice if we could live as one.
When will all this anger, hate and bigotry be done?"
– Ozzy Osbourne, "Dreamer"

Barbara Coloroso expands on Randel's theme that victims are targets because they are different in some way. The new child, the youngest child, the poor child, the rich child, the effeminate child, the physical or emotionally handicapped child, even the child who had the misfortune to be at the wrong place at the wrong time when a bully felt the need to be aggressive with someone, right at that moment.

A closer examination of school violence often reveals that victims either do not believe adults will help them or do not believe that adults can help them. Since bullying is not normally observed by adults, the victim fears he or she will not be believed by adults, especially if the bully is popular with peers. Tragically, for some victims, adults either condone bullying or actually participate in it by omission.

Bullycide is the term used when children kill themselves because they cannot face one more day of being bullied (Coloroso, p 54). In March of 1994, fifteen-year-old Brian Head walked calmly into his economics classroom, put a pistol to his temple and announced, "I can't take this anymore," and pulled the trigger. His mother told investigators that Brian had been bullied for many years. The unceasing attacks by his peers steadily broke his spirit and destroyed all his sense of self. His crime that made him a target? He liked to write poetry. Brian Head gave himself the death penalty for being different from other boys his age.

The term "bullycide" has been criticized by legal analysts because it suggests that the bully was personally responsible for the victim's death. In Brian's case, no bully pulled the trigger; Brian did. While the bully (or bullies) could face charges of physical assault and/or harassment, to hold the bully criminally liable for Brian's death seems a real stretch of criminal law. "Homicide" refers to one person intentionally, and with premeditation, killing another person. "Suicide" refers to killing oneself. One interpretation of "bullycide," then, is that the bully intentionally and with premeditation killed the victim he or she was bullying. The criminalization of bullying is being seriously considered by many state legislatures. This concept will be reviewed in a later chapter. For now, bullycide represents the ultimate response of a school-age child when bullying is either undetected or is ineffectively dealt with by adults when it is detected.

The Forensic Profile of a Bystander

Scaglione and Scaglione (2006) make the crucial point that bystanders provide support for the actions of the bully. Bystanders are sometimes referred to as "the silent majority." Coloroso (2003 p 65) emphatically states that there is no such thing as an "innocent bystander." This concept is prominent in a statement by Dr. Martin Luther King, Jr:

"In the end, we'll remember not the words of our enemies, but the silence of our friends."

The following is a communication between a therapist and an adolescent client:

NOTES OF A THERAPIST

Client: I hated it when they picked on Bobby. They called him fat, ugly, queer, just about anything you can think of. They only did it because people were watching and cheering them on. They made me sick.

Therapist: What did you do?

Client: Didn't do anything. What could I do? I didn't laugh or anything like that, but I didn't try to stop them either.

Therapist: Why not?

Client: You don't know these guys. If I'd said anything, they would have turned on me. I can't handle that. I need to make my grades so I can go to college.

Therapist: Do you think the victim could handle it?

Client: No, I guess not. But he was used to being picked on. I wasn't. I couldn't risk it. I still had to go to that school.

It is estimated that 75 to 80 percent of school-age students are aware of, or directly witness, bullying behavior but do nothing to stop it. Like the client above, the students fear retaliation by the bully or bullies. This applies to both male and female bullies and bystanders. In addition to fear of retaliation, bystanders have no clear concept of what they can and should do about bullying. If the school has no policy on bullying, the bystanders have no adult guidance. They fear that if they report bullying, they may inadvertently make things worse for the victim. Thus, the overall profile of the bystander is one that is fearful of retaliation and has no guidance for how to end the bullying. In their uncertainty and fear, they remain silent – not from choice, but from fear and ignorance. The victims are left to fend for themselves. The bystanders engage in acts of omission, not commission. Scaglione and Scaglione assert that bullies interpret the silence of bystanders as approval of their actions. Silence is interpreted as consent and approval. The bully, after all, seeks the bystanders' approval and at the same time their actions issue a subliminal warning: "This could be you."

Bystanders pay a high price for their silence. They know that a sense of fair play has been lost or ignored. Their self-confidence is eroded because of their passivity in not opposing the bully. Feelings of guilt increase each time they remain silent about the victim's torment. Bystanders deliberately choose to abandon their personal ethics in the interest of self-preservation. Young school-age children lack the cognitive ability to recognize the impact of their actions or non-actions on themselves and the victims of bullying. They do know right from wrong, and are able to categorize bullying as being wrong; they also understand that their non-action is also wrong. What young bystanders lack is clear direction from adults about what they can and should do when they witness bullying. Without this direction, bystanders' fear and lack of skills turn into apathy and feelings of helplessness.

Barbara Coloroso classifies bystanders as: (1) Followers who take an active part in the bullying but do not start it, (2) Supporters, or passive bystanders, who support the bullying but do not take an active part, (3) Passive supporters who like to watch the bullying but take no active part, (4) Disengaged onlookers who watch what is happening but do not take a stand, (5) Possible defenders who are disturbed by bullying and believe they ought to help, but do not, or (6) Defenders of the target who dislike bullying and try to help the victim. She further includes how the bystanders resolve to themselves why they do not intervene:

- This is not my fight. It is not my problem.

- The bully is my friend. The victim is not my friend.

- The victim is a loser, anyway. He or she had it coming.

- *Omerta*, the law of silence, prevails.

- It is better to be in the bully's in-group than to defend the victims and become a victim.

Bystanders to bullying are, in most cases, not cruel and uncaring school children. It is fear and ignorance that keeps them silent. In most cases, they would gladly have nothing further to do with bullies and bullying. Providing them with knowledge, support, and a way out can make all the difference in how they deal with bullying behavior by others.

Author and attorney Mary Jo McGrath (2007) discusses the complex role of the bystander within the culture of the school. She notes that bystanders participate in bullying with behavior ranging from active collusion in the bullying to fear about what they are observing. Not only do they fear becoming victims themselves, they also believe they have no power to stop the bullying. McGrath categorizes four types of bystanders:

FOUR TYPES OF BYSTANDERS	
Sidekicks	Join in the bullying
Reinforcers	Laugh and encourage the bullying

FOUR TYPES OF BYSTANDERS	
Outsiders	Do not take sides but distances themselves and remain silent
Defenders	Comfort the victim and try to stop the bullying

The following is a communication that occurred between a therapist and a thirteen-year-old girl who was a bystander/witness to a serious bullying incident where the victim was beaten so badly, she was admitted to the hospital. Assault and battery charges were brought against the bully.

NOTES OF A THERAPIST

Therapist: So why do you think this happened?

Client: I don't know. I mean, Cheryl (not her real name) was always getting picked on for being poor and not having stylish clothes and stuff. She always had a glob of snot coming out of her nose. I don't know why it went so far this time. It just happened. It was like Angie (not her real name) just lost it. She had picked on Cheryl before, but never like this. She was so angry.

Therapist: Are you afraid of Angie?

Client: I am now.

Therapist: Why is that?

Client: Angie has a lot of friends that back her up. If I testify against her, my ass is toast. If Angie doesn't get me back, her friends will. I know what happened was wrong, but what was I supposed to do, jump in there and get beat myself?

Therapist: Are you going to testify?

Client: No.

Therapist: How do you feel about your decision?

Client: I feel like crap about it. But what good would it do? It won't change what happened.

NOTES OF A THERAPIST

Therapist: No, but it might help you feel better about yourself.

Client: It also might get me killed.

Conclusion

Bullies, victims, and bystanders have very complex inter-relationships. One without the others cannot exist alone. Thus, changing the actions, thoughts, and values of one will bring about some sort of changes in the others. Operating as a distorted, opportunistic, and dysfunctional triumvirate, each exists because the others exist as well. Looking back into history, we see this same pattern age after age; dictatorships, serial homicides, armed conflicts – in each of these, there must be "supporting players" for historical pathology to have existed. Nazi Germany, Stalin's genocide, the fall of the Russian Tzars and the birth of communism, the Charles Manson "family" of murderers, and the brutal rule of Saddam Hussein; these historical tragic dramas could not have played out if even one key person, group, or society was not part of the "recipe." Within the microcosm of the school, these patterns occur prolifically because all three key persons play their roles to perfection, whether they truly wish to or not. If the children involved in these triads of unspeakable emotional and physical injury know no other way to interact with others, the tragic recipe is complete.

"You did what you knew how to do at the time.
When you knew better, you did better."
– Maya Angelou

Remember

04.28.1999 — Taber, Alberta, Canada

One student killed, one wounded at W. R. Myers High School. The suspect, a 14-year-old boy, had dropped out of school after he was severely ostracized by his classmates.

chapter six

Myth-Busting: The Truth Behind Bullying

Introduction

School-age children, like many adults, do what they know how to do, what they have the opportunity to do, and what they are rewarded in some way for doing. People do what works for them. Most of the time, children's behavior conforms to what they are taught by their emotionally healthy adult role models. In a perfect world, all families would be positive role models for their children. This ideal is far from the truth, however. Some children bully others with aggressive speech and behavior because that is what happens in their homes. When family disputes are settled with fists and/or weapons, this is how children of these homes learn to solve problems with others. When parents set no limits and boundaries on their children, they do not learn self-control. When parents are passive about social injustice, their children fail to learn to assertively speak against that which is wrong, i.e. bullying behavior by their peers. When parents either do not know the truth about bullies, victims, and bystanders, or when they would rather believe that the truth is not the truth, their children learn that they need not take responsibility for their actions.

The first step in eliminating bullying in America's schools is to first acknowledge that bullying not only exists in our schools, but that it is causing inestimable destruction of our children, whether they are the bullies, the victims, or the bystanders. Lifting the veil of ignorance, breaking the silence of *omerta*, and empowering children to become bully-proof are the only ways this psychological warfare will end.

Myth Busting

Mary Jo McGrath, an education and personnel law attorney and professional development specialist, founded the SUCCEED system of eliminating bullying that focuses on adult leaders' steps of thinking, listening, speaking, acting. School leaders should ask four fundamental questions about a bullying incident:

- What happened?

- What apparent harm did it cause?

- What is known about anything preceding the event that contributed to the situation?

- What, if any, immediate action should be taken?

McGrath notes that, before this or any other method of removing bullying from schools can succeed, the truth must be told about this practice, and adults must accept these truths. One has only to research the incidents of school violence, of which the Columbine shootings were only the beginning, and the number of children who have emotional breakdowns and/or commit bullycide to be convinced that how we think, feel, and react to bullying must change. All that is required is that adults – parents and educators – acknowledge the truth about bullying and formulate plans to eliminate it in schools.

First, educators must understand the fallacy of the myth, "We don't have bullying in our school."

Public schools, private schools, urban schools, inner-city schools, rural schools – all are places where children go to be educated, not fight for their physical and emotional health. Parents and educators should demand more for their tax dollars, like safety and zero tolerance for bullying. The only school where bullying is not an issue is home schooling. Bullying is widespread in the United States and internationally. Teachers and school administrators rarely see it occurring, but it would be foolish to draw the conclusion that since bullying is not observed by adults or reported by victims and bystanders that it does not happen. We do not observe the flu virus finding entry into our bodies, but that hardly means it does not happen; some strains of the flu are deadly. This myth that "because we did not see it happen, it did not happen" can be just as deadly as the flu when it infects vulnerable people.

In 2004, researchers at UCLA conducted a field study over a two-week period with diverse groups of 192 sixth-graders in Los Angeles schools. In one school, 46 percent reported that they were bullied during the survey period, and 42 to 66 percent reported witnessing bullying (Nishina & Juvonen, 2005a). Neither the size of the school nor actual class sizes make a difference in whether or not bullying occurs in a particular school.

CASE STUDY: ROSE D.

Rose is a twelve-year-old girl who was brought to the mental health clinic by her mother because Rose "won't stop crying, she won't eat, and she can't sleep. She won't tell me what's the matter with her. Her daddy's just about had it." Rose agreed to speak with the therapist alone.

CASE STUDY: ROSE D.

When asked what was troubling her, Rose began to weep softly but profusely, but did not speak. Eventually, Rose wiped her eyes and sat up straight, saying, "I'm ready now." Rose stated that she is considering suicide, and that she had a plan to sneak out of the house late at night and hang herself from a tree in a nearby park. When asked what was causing these suicidal thoughts, Rose stated that she could not go to school because "they're at me every day, and I can't take it no more."

Rose and her family are originally from the Appalachian mountains of Tennessee. She has three younger siblings: an eight-year-old brother and twin sisters, age five. Until last year, Rose and her family lived in impoverished conditions in Appalachia until her father decided to join the military "to get steady work." Rose had never attended formal schooling until she was enrolled in the public school closest to where her father was stationed. After testing, she was placed in the fifth grade; it was determined that she was academically unable to be placed with students her own age. She stated that "ever since that first day, all they could do was poke fun at me. The way I talk, my clothes, I don't know the things they know like about movie stars and music and stuff like that 'cause we didn't have TV where we lived. They was all younger than me, too. I guess I was just too far different from them and I didn't fit in."

Rose began to be regularly bullied by two other girls in her class who called her "dumb hillbilly," and "Miss Fashion Model." The girls took great care not to be overheard by any adults, but many of the other girls in her class, and a few of the boys, were present when these things were said, and looked forward to "Rose time" during lunch and recess. Rose recounted an incident in the school cafeteria when one of the girls deliberately spilled gravy on Rose's dress saying, "There, now your clothes are just as dirty as you are. Don't you people take baths?" Rose stated that her family was very religious; she told her mother about this incident, and her mother said "It musta been God's will."

A few months later, Rose began to have menstrual periods. Both girls that were bullying her stole her purse; finding some sanitary napkins in it, they threw the napkins all around the schoolyard, shouting, "Rose

CASE STUDY: ROSE D.

is a bleeder!" Since Rose had been taught that personal feminine hygiene was very private, she was horribly embarrassed by this incident. Since that time, the two girls kept asking her, "Hey Rose, you bleeding again?" The boys in her class began saying this to her as well.

Rose then discussed the fifth grade school Christmas play; the entire class was taking part except Rose. She stated, "My daddy don't believe in presents and plays and songs and stuff. He says that Jesus died because we all sinned, so we shouldn't be laughing on his birthday. He says that the only good way of thanking Jesus for what he done for us was to read the Bible all Christmas day."

Rose stated that she liked her teacher, Mrs. B. She asked Mrs. B. one time what would happen if "kids in our class got picked on." Mrs. B. told Rose that this sort of behavior would not be tolerated. "But it did happen every day to me and nobody did anything about it."

By this time, Rose was losing weight because she was always anxious and nauseous. She was not sleeping well, had nightmares, and felt tired most of the time. She had no friends and spent her time after school helping her mother care for the younger children. The incident that brought Rose to the clinic happened four days earlier. Rose's parents did not allow her to wear slacks; her family believed women should always wear dresses. Rose was wearing a hand-made dress that her mother had sewn especially for her; Rose stated the dress was beautiful, with pink and yellow roses in the material. When the girl who sat behind her in class noticed that the dress was hand-stitched in the back, she stuck a pencil into one of the seams and ripped it, causing a large hole in the back of the dress. The rest of the class laughed at her even though Mrs. B. told them to be quiet.

At recess, Mrs. B. took Rose into the school office where she repaired the dress with a sewing kit. She changed Rose's seat to the front row next to her desk. On the way home from school, the two girls who were bullying her and several other boys and girls from her class caught up with her as she walked home, and smeared the dress with dirt and mud. Rose began screaming and ran home. She could not stop crying and would not eat.

CASE STUDY: ROSE D.

She decided to commit suicide because her father would not allow her to leave the school. "No more," Rose told the therapist, "I can't handle it no more. I know Jesus would be angry if I killed myself, but I have to. Nobody cares or understands. Mrs. B. is nice, but she don't have to be me every day. I don't think she knows how bad things were because everyone was nice to me when she was there. Daddy told me to hush crying. Mama said it was all God's will. I might as well be dead."

Another myth that McGrath dispels is that there are many more important safety issues at school other than bullying. According to a combination of research studies, 160,000 children each day miss school because they do not feel safe. Adults rarely attribute this fear to bullying; gangs, drugs, weapons, and racism are of far greater concern. Yet in 2003, 6 percent of students ages 12 to 18 missed school for fear of being attacked on the way to and from school by others who were bullying them (National Center for Education Statistics, 2005b).

A particularly disturbing and dangerous myth is that teachers see everything and respond quickly when bullying occurs. Rose's story clearly indicates that this is not the case, as do the ever-increasing numbers of school shooting and suicides. McGrath points out that teachers do not have eyes in the back of their heads, nor do they accompany every child to and from school. Statistical variations belie the accuracy of teachers' reports; McGrath reports that 75 percent of teachers believe that they are aware of bullying, and that they respond quickly to stop it; only 25 percent of students report that teachers observe and stop bullying. It seems obvious that teachers, however well-meaning, simply cannot observe and stop actions that are carefully hidden from them any more than law enforcement personnel can observe and stop every crime that is committed.

There may be teachers in our schools that are more observant than most, and do act swiftly if they observe bullying. However, they are clearly outnumbered by the student population, especially those who bully and the bystanders who do not report what they see.

Other stereotypical myths are that bullies are social outcasts with very low self-esteems who bully others for attention and power. They make others feel bad so that they can feel good. McGrath cites research that indicates the contrary; bullies' popularity among their peers ranges from above average to slightly below average. Of course, excelling at sports or making high grades certainly does not predict that such a child is or will become a bully. Nor does the lack of these talents predict bullying behavior. Regardless of grades and degree of success at extracurricular activities, any child has the capability to become a bully if other circumstances discussed in the previous chapter are present. Most bullies think well of themselves rather than being anxious and insecure. Low self-esteem and lack of popularity may seem to be logical reasons for a child to bully, but this is a false premise not holding up to the scrutiny of the research. Unless parents and educators alter their vision of a bully's self-esteem and popularity, they will miss identifying the confident, popular bullies.

Bullying is not limited to "obvious" students – yet another myth/stereotype unsupported by research findings. They are not as easy to identify as we would like to believe. Most adults, when asked to envision the "class bully" and describe that student, would most likely conjure an image of a male student who is socially inept, disliked, is bigger and tougher than other students, makes poor grades, comes from an impoverished and/or dysfunctional home, is physically unattractive, and is universally feared by all students who are younger and smaller. Nor is it impossible to detect the early warning signs that a student is a bully or is being bullied. Previous chapters discussed very clear signs and symptoms of bullies, victims, and bystanders. Again, it must be emphasized that bullying is a "silent assault." The early warning signs of bullying are easily identified if adults abandon the myths and stereotypes.

Perhaps the most dangerous myth is that there is no correlation between bullying and extreme violence. Sexual serial killer Jeffrey Dahmer was a frequent target of bullying in school. Very immature for his age, Dahmer was teased about his learning disabilities and his lack of social skills. In his school, doing something that is goofy or annoying was called "doing a Dahmer." This is the label under which Dahmer was bullied; not content to merely call him names or physically intimidate him, his classmates invented a whole new genre of social ineptness and stupidity that bore his name. Jeffrey Dahmer went on as an adult to commit some of the most atrocious homicides and deviant cannibalistic behavior that this country has ever experienced. America heard Dahmer's expression of remorse for his crimes, which had the ring of sincerity. Perhaps, before he became a killer, he was first a victim of bullying. When Dahmer was killed in prison by another inmate, the nation breathed a sigh of relief that something vile, horrific, and not quite human had left this world. No one could have predicted that Dahmer would, as an adult, commit these truly ghastly crimes simply because he was bullied as a child. This was but one element of the "recipe" that created what Jeffrey Dahmer became.

When Eric Harris and Dylan Klebold killed 15 people, including themselves, and wounded 21 more at Columbine High School in 1999, a "wake-up call" sounded in schools across the nation:

Bullying is not child's play, it is not humorous, and it is not harmless. Their rampage stemmed from years of bullying, rejection, and abuse by their peer group. Their legacy of extreme violence continues. On March 7, 2001, Elizabeth Bush, age fourteen, took her father's pistol into the school cafeteria in Williamsport, PA and shot head cheerleader Jodie Morse. Elizabeth was a quiet, religious girl who abhorred violence and put up posters of Mother Teresa and Martin Luther King, Jr. in her bedroom, along with pictures of the victims at Columbine. Elizabeth wanted to either become a human rights activist or a nun. Because of her passivity, Elizabeth was threatened and teased by her classmates, including Jodie Morse. She countered being bullied with extreme violence.

As discussed earlier, there is no direct causal factor between being bullied and committing first degree murder or suicide. Human behavior is way too complex to attribute deviant violent behavior solely to being bullied. Not every child who is bullied becomes a killer. Not every killer was bullied as a child. Yet in extreme cases of school violence, bullying is nearly always a factor. An investigation by the U.S. Secret Service of 37 school shootings from 1974 to 2000 revealed that 71 percent of the shooters were subjected to severe, long-term bullying behavior that left them feeling persecuted and threatened. The investigation suggested that school shootings can be prevented if bullying in schools was targeted as "zero tolerance" behavior.

The most puzzling myth about bullying is that it is not a legal issue, but a character issue. Children who bully should not be taken into the juvenile justice system, but instead need merely counseling to improve their character. By definition, an act of juvenile delinquency is behavior that, if committed by an adult, would be considered as a crime. Adults who commit an assault and battery will find themselves standing before a criminal court judge and jury to account for their actions. When bullies pushed Andy Williams' head into a toilet and tried to set him on fire, questions were raised as to why their actions did not constitute battering, punishable through the juvenile justice system. In many cases, bullying crosses the line between annoying harassment and criminal behavior. If McGrath and others have their way, persistent bullying behavior will be legally actionable around the nation.

Conclusion

A machine that is broken cannot be fixed until the problem is identified and corrected. Bullying is a "social machine" that will remain broken until parents and educators acknowledge several research-established facts: Bullying occurs in most, if not all, schools across America in varying degrees of viciousness and longevity. Adults cannot possibly witness and stop all incidents of bullying. Many children do not feel safe at school because of bullying. Bullies come in all age groups, rarely have self-esteem issues, may be popular with peers, and are at least average in academic performance. Early warning signs that a child is bullying others can be detected by those who wish to see. Most disturbing is the fact that school violence and victims of bullying have, in the majority of cases, a connection in varying degrees.

Dr. Phillip C. McGraw states in his book *Life Strategies* (2002) that "you can't fix what you don't acknowledge." If parents and adults continue to accept myths and stereotypes about bullies and their victims instead of acknowledging the facts as proven in countless research studies, there will be more Columbine-like occurrences. Under the auspices of this theory, bullying might be eliminated by empowering victims and bystanders to speak out in non-violent ways to end this nightmare from which America cannot seem to awaken.

"Those who do not remember the past are condemned to repeat it."
— F. Nietzsche

Remember

12.01.1997 — West Paducah, Kentucky

Michael Carneal, 14, killed three students and wounded five others as they participated in a prayer circle at Heath High School.

Section 3

3

Solutions for Parents, Teachers, Victims, and Bystanders

Remember
03.05.2001 — Santee, California
Charles Andrew Williams, 15, killed two killed and wounded 13 at Santana
High School.

chapter seven

Creating Bully-Proof Children and Bully-Busting in Your Home

Introduction

Step by step. Parent by parent. Teacher by teacher. School by school. Child by child.

This is how bully-proof children are created. Not with an amazing epiphany that enlightens the country about the often irreversible harm created by bullying. Not with an equally amazing epiphany by the bully that his or her behavior is destructive for others. Not by invoking the death penalty for bullies. Not even by making this book a selection of Oprah's Book Club. Not by anything as easy as these "solutions." Creating bully-proof children is much more difficult than it seems within the pages of a book or an hour-long talk show. Since bullying involves much more than just the bully him or herself, creating bully-proof children must also take into account and bring about changes in social systems, such as families, educators, counselors, law enforcement, bullies, victims, and bystanders. If it takes a village to raise a child, it takes a nation to save one.

Several objectives are involved in bully-proofing school-age children:

- Throw wide open the doors of communication between children, their peers, and adults regarding bullying. Shine the brightest spotlight on this issue and defeat forever the *omerta* that allows bullying to continue.

- Take away the bully's audience; empower bystanders in refusing to take part, silently watch, and not report bullying.

- Deal directly with the bully, refusing to accept his or her denial of culpability.

- Teach victims to use their natural strengths and learned behavior to assertively refuse to become victims of bullying. Teach them to solve the problem rather than simply solving it for them.

- Parents, educators, and other adults must act to prevent bullying, as well as react to it when it occurs.

Accomplishing these goals is but one step in creating bully-proof children. Nevertheless, it is a good and necessary step. It is the beginning of the beginning; when American schools implement a "zero tolerance" policy for bullying, developing that policy starts here.

"What we have here is a failure to communicate"

This line from the classic prison movie, *Cool Hand Luke*, captures the essence of why and how bullying is allowed to proliferate in our schools. Quite simply, no one is talking. The bullies certainly are not; they want to continue their behavior with impunity. The victims are not; they have been conditioned by society to "suck it up" and "be a man."

Scaglione and Scaglione believe that the key to ending bullying is opening communication between children and other children, teachers to children, parents to children, children to teachers, and children to parents. Non-communication among all these key players perpetuates bullying, just as it did on *The Andy Griffith Show*. Previous chapters explained why and how bullying becomes a "silent assault." Once the cat is out of the bag, it is impossible to get it back inside. Thus, once a child reports being bullied, adults must openly discuss the matter with these children; the bell cannot be un-rung. Sheriff Taylor's advice to Opie about physically defending himself is not going to solve America's immense bullying problem; massive fistfights all over the country is not the answer, although it may seem like the simplest answer.

Communication between adults and children about being bullied requires a lot more listening by the adult than it does talking. Before jumping to solutions that have not been well thought out and which could make the problem worse, adults must hear the child out completely and indicate that the child *has been heard*. Knowing this will help make bullied children much more comfortable and hopeful in further disclosing his/her victimization by a bully. Scaglione and Scaglione recommend five "don'ts" in listening to a child talk about being bullied:

- Don't minimize or make light of the bullying described.

- Don't laugh.

- Don't get angry.

- Don't say, "I'll take care of that!"

- Don't give advice – this will come later.

Adults' initial response to a child's disclosure of bullying is crucial. To establish trust with the adult, the child needs for the adult to be calm, using reflective listening techniques that echo back what the child has said. For example, an adult might respond, "What I hear you saying is that for the past month, Angie has been spreading untrue gossip about you to all the kids in your class, and you're really upset by this because it has happened several times in the past." Adults should ask questions in a sensitive, non-accusatory manner: "I'd like to hear more about what has been happening to you and how these incidents make you feel." A child's disclosure of being bullied is not an interrogation. More questions may come at a later time after the adult earns the child's trust. The initial communication should be merely a validation that the child has been heard, understood, and believed. Parents and teachers must respond to the child's disclosure in a way that does not make an already fearful and anxious child even more so. Reassurance that the child has done the right thing by disclosing the bullying is also crucial; it is important that the child hears that the bullying is not his or her fault, that they are no longer alone with this secret, and that help is on the way.

The May 2007 edition of *Redbook* magazine contains an article by Ellen Welty on bullying — specifically, how mothers can communicate with the bully's mother. Welty discusses four helpful ways for parents to talk with a child who discloses that he or she is being bullied:

- "I'm here for you." Although the bully makes the victim feel helpless and alone, parents can let the child know that he or she is no longer alone and suffering.

- "It's not your fault." It is the bully's behavior that needs to change, not the victim's behavior. Bullies often tell the victim the many reasons he or she deserves to be bullied, e.g. "You're dumb," "You're a fag," "You're poor," "Your clothes look stupid," "You're ugly," and so many more. The bully is only fulfilling a natural role.

- "I'd be upset if that happened to me." Isolating the victim from sources of help and comfort is a bully's specialty. Already vulnerable, the victim is convinced that if he or she revealed the truth, other kids would mark the victim as being different in some way.

- "Let's see what we can do." It is only natural that parents want to "fix" things for their children, as previously discussed. However, victims of bullies do not want a parent to stop the bully; they want to do so, and need parents to teach them how. In addition, they are comforted by knowing that they no longer must try to handle the problem on their own.

Regardless of the wonderful humor of *The Andy Griffith Show*, it is not helpful to bully-proof a child through teaching him or her to hit back. In Mayberry, everything was funny – from the bumbling antics of Deputy Barney Fife to "town drunk" Otis Campbell. However, this is not Mayberry; when a child is being bullied while others watch, no director yells, "Cut!" Young, elementary school-age children tend to believe what they are told, from the reality of Santa Claus to the crime-stopping skills of Superman. They also believe what they are told about themselves. For example, if a child is bullied by being habitually called "stupid," "Forrest Gump," or a "loser," the child will most likely believe that these are accurate descriptions. As the child grows into adulthood, that stereotypic label goes along for the ride, causing an abysmally low self-esteem. Scholastic failures, occupational difficulties, and lack of interpersonal relationships will be the inevitable result. In Mayberry, it took only 30 minutes, including commercials, for Andy to bully-proof Opie. In our towns and homes, it takes much more time and effort.

"Nobody can make you feel inferior without your consent."
— Eleanor Roosevelt

Scaglione and Scaglione state that "the best armor parents and teachers can outfit children with is to feel good about themselves." If parents wait, either from lack of watchfulness or by lack of knowledge about bullying, until a child has been bullied for a substantial period of time to prepare the child for coping with bullies, it is too late for early intervention and the bell cannot be un-rung. This does not mean that these children cannot recover emotionally from being bullied; they can, and for the most part, they do. The sooner damage control begins, the better the outcome.

It is not in the best interests of the child to take him or her to that brink unarmed with coping strategies at all. Preparing children to cope with bullies should begin long before they ever face one at school. Preparation involves raising children to be independent, self-sufficient, assertive, and skilled in problem solving. Children who are raised with praise, compliments, encouragement, empowerment to solve problems, and respect for themselves and others are well prepared for the taunts and intimidations of a bully. Teaching children at a young age that although they, like everyone else, are not perfect but put forth their best efforts enables them to learn that they can handle criticism, being teased, and called names. They do not give the fledgling bully what he/she wants; they do not overreact or become more vulnerable. School bullies are only the beginning. As children grow into adulthood, they must face bullying in the workplace, political bullies, even bullies in their own homes and families. Given the choice, the workplace and domestic bullies will always look for the co-worker, the subordinate, the spouse, and the child who allows him or her to control and intimidate him.

CASE STUDY: PEARL B.

Pearl came to the mental health clinic for help with depression and substance abuse. She is a military officer who is the senior officer in charge of her section, and has both officers, enlisted, and civilian subordinates. She has been stationed at her current location for only six months.

Pearl stated that her occupational stress is "enormous" and that she has become depressed because of it. She has been drinking heavily to cope with feelings of shame, rage, fear, and hopelessness. Pearl has no prior mental health or substance abuse history. She began her story by detailing the emotional abuse she copes with on a daily basis; her subordinates disrespect her publicly, they complain "up the chain" to her flight and squadron commanders about every thing from the kind of music she listens to and her outspoken manner.

She believes that her superior officers think poorly of her and "would like to get rid of me." Pearl brought with her a large file of documents that seemed to support her fears, such as a copy of the daily log that her subordinates were keeping about her, a copy of the paperwork firing a civilian employee who liked Pearl, a large quantity of "memos for record" that her subordinates wrote about her behaviors that they did not like, and a copy of her recent performance report from her superior stating that her duty performance was not acceptable, but gave her no previous notice that her duty performance was sub-standard.

Pearl discussed her situation with the installation's commander;

CASE STUDY: PEARL B.

because of the investigation of her complaint, her superiors were not promoted, one civilian was fired, one junior officer was sent to another installation, and another junior officer left the military. Pearl stated that she had a "major meltdown" because she could no longer cope with the occupational stress because "now everyone hates me because I told the truth."

Pearl's treatment plan included receiving antidepressant medication and a cessation of alcohol use. Pearl discussed her childhood by calling it "a disaster." She was an only child and was generally held in high regard by her parents. However, Pearl recalls that in the sixth grade she began to be regularly teased and taunted by a boy in her class, Steven. Pearl stated that she was tall for her age, very thin, and had bad acne. Steven called her names in front of the other kids like "slats," "Godzilla," "pimples," "dopey," "scarecrow," and "zit-face."

Pearl had always made good grades in school, but after the bullying began, her grades began to drop and she was punished at home; she did not tell her parents about the bullying. Steven threatened to "slap your gross-looking face" unless she did all of his homework for him; she complied not because she was afraid of Steven, but because she hoped the bullying would stop. Steven's taunts escalated into profanity; he called her a "skinny bitch" and a "disgusting whore."

Pearl stated that because her parents were "nice people," they would not know what she should do about Steven so she did not tell them. Steven then insisted that Pearl do the homework for two of his friends, and again Pearl complied. She was dismayed when she learned that Steven was in several seventh grade classes with her. "He started in right away, making me do his and his friends' homework, giving him money, and saying embarrassing and humiliating things about me in front of other kids."

Pearl found out that Steven had written graffiti about her in one of the boys' bathrooms; "Pearl does everybody." She stated that after this, she felt she could not go to school any longer, and she began to skip classes. When her parents found out, they punished her and made her go to school.

CASE STUDY: PEARL B.

Steven's sexual bullying intensified; he rubbed his crotch against her in the crowded hallways, and touched her breasts. Once he reached up her skirt and touched her vaginal area through her underwear, then sniffed his fingers and said, "Good smell. Anybody want some? Zit-face here puts out for anybody."

Pearl stated that the next day she told her mother that she would kill herself if she had to go to school with Steven; she finally told her mother about the bullying. Pearl's mother was outraged. She immediately called the school principal, and she and Pearl went to talk with him. Steven was expelled from school, and Pearl started attending another school.

When asked how this bullying affected her today, Pearl said, "I believe anything negative that is said about me. I do not know how to stand up for myself. I let all those kids do that to me." Although Pearl's parents believed her about the bullying, they did not seem to know what to do about it. "They got Steven away from me, but didn't help me with my emotional problems because they didn't know how." She believes that her current occupational problems are caused by her low self-esteem. "I hate myself because I'm letting it happen all over again. I'm back in the sixth grade. I hate all these people, but I hate myself more."

Talk About the Hippo

Among psychotherapists, the analogy of the hippo in the living room is frequently used to help break down the denial of a problem and acknowledge that something needs to be done about the problem. This vignette involves the presence of a baby hippo in a family's living room. This would be a problem for most families. However, when a family member has a secret that is never talked about, it becomes a hippo in the living room. The more the hippo is surrounded by silence and denial, the more it grows into a very large hippo. Naturally, this large hippo makes a terrible mess, but no one says anything about it. Once a family member says, "Hey, what are we going to do about this messy hippo in our living room?" then the denial either strengthens – "What hippo? I don't see any hippo. You're nuts." Or the hippo's presence must be acknowledged and dealt with. When a child is bullied, is a bully, or is a bystander in bullying, this very large hippo must be dealt with via head-on communication. It is the adult's responsibility to calmly but thoroughly respond to the child's disclosure, offer understanding and validation, and let the child know that this hippo will soon be vacating the child's living room.

Empowering Bystanders

Barbara Coloroso believes that bystanders play a crucial role in bully-proofing children. Bullies carefully hide their actions from adults, but they like to play to a full house of supportive, jeering bystanders. Ideally, bystanders can show bullies that they will not be admired for their cruel actions, nor will their behavior be condoned or tolerated. Instead of remaining silent witnesses, bystanders can become very vocal witnesses. In this manner, the bully loses his or her supporters and audience, and each bystander has the potential to become an enemy. Coloroso suggests six ways that parents can empower bystanders to become a force for eliminating bullying rather than condoning it:

SIX WAYS PARENTS CAN EMPOWER BYSTANDERS	
1	Intervene immediately with appropriate discipline. Children must understand that being a silent bystander to cruelty is morally wrong.

	SIX WAYS PARENTS CAN EMPOWER BYSTANDERS
2	Create opportunities for the child to "do good." This may include helping another child with homework, volunteering in the community, and many other philanthropic activities. Teach the child that helping others is a key to their happiness and self-esteem.
3	Nurture empathy. In a non-accusatory manner, ask the bystander, "Think about how you would feel if you were bullied and no one stepped forward to help you."
4	Teach age-appropriate friendship skills that are assertive, respectful, and peaceful rather than being centered on power, control, and fearful silence.
5	Encourage the child to participate in constructive, entertaining, and energizing activities. There is no room for the bully in these kinds of activities. Provide the child with much more satisfying and pleasant activity.
6	Teach the child to "will good" for others. Rather than being subjected to watching another child repeatedly treating others in a cruel manner, help the child focus on wanting other children to be happy and successful. The former bystander will develop an inner moral voice that guides him/her towards a life of sharing, caring, helping and serving.

Scaglione and Scaglione (2006) also recommend empowering bystanders of bullying. They emphasize that in order to bully-proof children and create an atmosphere of zero tolerance for bullying, *all* support, direct or indirect, must be taken away from the bully. Bullies do what they do because they *can*. They know that none of their "audience" members will intervene to stop the bullying. They like the powerful, dominant image that bullying creates among the bystanders.

In *The Wizard of Oz* Dorothy kills the Wicked Witch of the West without intending to by throwing water on the witch while her supposed minions watched. Much to everyone's astonishment, the witch's soldiers were actually happy and relieved that they were free from the witch's cruel domination. Ding-dong, the witch was dead! Bystanders of bullying react in much the same manner if "their" bully is stopped. Although they dare not say so at the time, the bystanders of school bullying are most commonly relieved and pleased that they no longer have to keep the secret of *omerta*, nor do they have to support the bully's actions out of fear. Lest we blame the child bystanders for supporting the bully in the first place, let it be remembered that the most vicious adult bullies in recorded history were able to continue their despicable actions because no one dared oppose them. Let us also refer to recent history, as the world coped with the brutal bullying of Saddam Hussein. Having true supporters (bystanders) small in number, Hussein was allowed to terrorize and murder hundreds of thousands of his own countrymen. The first Gulf War, which Hussein called "the mother of all battles," turned out to be the "mother of all surrenders" when his elite Republican Guard soldiers abandoned their posts and weapons and fled for their lives, surrendering to U.S. and NATO forces. When U.S.-led military forces deposed of Hussein through Operation Iraqi Freedom, countless Iraqis celebrated their own version of "ding-dong, the witch is dead." Hussein's execution may have been less important to the Iraqi bystanders than his disgrace and removal from power.

Taking this recent analogy even further, one of the myths about bullying, as defined by McGrath, is that bullies are frightened, insecure people, a notion that she disputes. Saddam Hussein fled from his attackers, hiding for days in a small hole in the ground, a loaded pistol at his side. When uprooted by U.S. Marines, Hussein surrendered without firing a shot. His sons died in a firefight with U.S. forces; their father, the feared bully, submitted meekly to his captors, his weapon still silent. Whether Hussein's actions were typical of a bully, or atypical, is left to the opinion of others and the judgment of history.

With their assertion that all support must be taken away from the bully, Scaglione and Scaglione recommend several crucial actions to accomplish this goal and to create bully-proof children, including bystanders:

- Involve all stakeholders: school staff, parents, and the community.

- Raise the level of awareness about bullying for all adults.

- Gain the commitment of the entire student body to make their school and themselves bully-proof.

- All should support the victim(s) and confront the bully.

- Continue to educate all stakeholders about bullying.

- Set very clear and immediate consequences for bullying.

- Provide a vigilant level of supervision of the school campus.

Scaglione and Scaglione also recommend some guidelines for parents on bully proofing their children that also serve as lessons about being a bystander to bullying:

- Educate children about bullying and how to cope with it.

- Promote and reward peaceful, positive behavior.

- Provide character education; instructions on kindness, respect, and responsibility.

- Teach assertiveness and conflict resolution social skills.

"The opposite of love is not hate, but indifference; indifference creates evil. Indifference is what allows evil to be strong, what gives it power."
— Elie Wiesel, Holocaust survivor

It is highly unlikely that a child is going to come home from school and announce, "Hey Mom and Dad guess what? Jimmy is bullying Ralph, and I watch." Even while they are doing it, bystanders know this is unacceptable behavior and are not likely to disclose it in a conversational manner.

One area that is lacking in the literature on bullying is how to induce a child to disclose that he or she has been a bystander to bullying. In reality, this may never happen, even if parents are fairly sure that their child is a bystander. There need not be a disclosure for parents to address bystanding and empowering their children to cease being a silent witness to cruelty. As Coloroso indicates, continuously emphasizing the need for kindness, fair play, respect, empathy, and conscience. Returning to Alfred Adler's concept of social interest, parents can prevent bystanding by instilling in their children the need and virtue of caring about what is going on around them in their school microcosm and becoming involved in the non-support of wrongdoing.

CASE STUDY: RICHARD G.

Richard is a 26 year-old man, unmarried with no children, who came to the mental health clinic for help with anger management. Richard described himself as "an angry guy who's pissed off most of the time." When asked by the therapist to describe some of the things that made him angry, Richard replied, "Just

CASE STUDY: RICHARD G.

about everything. People. The stupid things they do. They're lazy and ignorant. I just can't stand them. And other stuff, like things not working right. Computers, cars, phones, you name it. I get angry whenever any little thing doesn't go right."

Richard agreed that his perfectionist expectations were unrealistic. "That's why I'm here. I know it's wrong, and I know that it drives people away from me. I don't have any friends. I don't have a girlfriend. People stay away from me in droves because I'm mad all day, every day. Hell, I gave away my dog because she didn't like me either. People don't like me, and I don't like me. But I don't know how to stop being so angry all the time." Richard's personal history revealed that he came from an intact, "normal" home; his parents treated him with love, kindness, and discipline when needed. He has a brother, Tony, who is two years older. Richard did well in school and played high school football. He stated that he was not very out-going and had a few good friends, and went out on occasional dates. After graduation, Richard paid his way through college, earning a degree in forestry. He is currently employed as a supervisor of a fish and game reserve. He stated that the people he works with are afraid of his temper and rarely talk to him unless they have to. His own supervisor has counseled him about his anger and attitude towards others; Richard is afraid he will lose his job if he does not make changes in the way he interacts with others.

"That's not the only reason I'm here," he stated. "I'm tired of myself. I hate being this way and I don't get why I can't just be cool." After several therapy sessions, Richard discussed his relationship with his brother, Tony. Richard stated that he looked up to Tony.

"He has everything I want. A nice wife, three kids, a decent job, and friends to hang out with." Richard then stated that he has been angry with Tony for years, but has never talked with Tony about his anger. "When I was in the seventh grade, some guys started to pick on me and call me names. Fag, spaz, retard, village idiot, butt-ugly, stuff like that.

I ignored them, but they didn't stop and soon everybody, including a girl I liked, was laughing at me. Then these guys started punching me

CASE STUDY: RICHARD G.

in gym class, knocking me over and crap like that. Pretending to the teacher that it was an accident, yeah. They hit me in the face with a baseball once and laughed about it because I had stitches. They said not to worry about it because I was an ugly SOB to begin with. The thing was, Tony knew about all this. He even saw a lot of it, like the thing with the baseball. And he didn't do a damn thing about it. I wasn't going to beg him to help me, and I shouldn't have had to. He should have helped his younger brother. I'd help him if somebody was messing with him. Where was he? How would he like it if somebody was jerking one of his kids around and nobody helped? I just try to stay clear of Tony. If I even see him, it reminds me of what he didn't do."

In this case study, it is clear that Tony, a bystander to his brother being bullied, was the source of Richard's underlying anger. This was a "double betrayal." Not only was Tony a bystander to bullying, but the victim was his own brother. Most bystanders to bullying fail to understand the crucial role they play in allowing the bullying to occur and perpetuate. Coloroso wrote, "Since much of the bullying goes on "under the radar" of adults, a potent force is kids themselves showing bullies that they will not be looked up to, nor will their cruel behavior be condoned or tolerated." In Richard's eyes, Tony failed to discharge these responsibilities.

Bully-Proofing Your Child: The Lowdown

Derek Randel, nationally known parent coach and former teacher, wrote in *Stopping School Violence* (2006) that bullying and school violence will never completely stop, but it can be reduced significantly.

> "People treat you the way you teach them to treat you."
> – Jack Canfield

"We teach people how to treat us."
– Dr. Phillip C. McGraw

There must be something to these statements since there are so many like them. Since bullying can begin at such a young age, e.g. elementary school, parents may be at a loss to convey this concept to their six-year-old. Randel cuts through the haze of literature about bully-proofing children and recommends the following teaching essentials:

- Encourage your child to report being bullied to you. Children have the right to feel safe.

- Validate your child's feelings. Feelings of sadness, hurt, and anger are normal.

- Rather than rushing into solutions, ask your child how he or she has attempted to solve the problem.

- Ask questions that encourage your child to think. "Do you have an idea how this problem could be solved?"

- Stress the importance of body language. Teach your child how to behave with self-confidence.

- Teach problem-solving skills that can be used when your child is being bullied, such as communicating intolerance of being a victim.

- Coach your child in alternatives, like avoidance of the bully by being involved in many social activities near an adult.

- Involve your child in activities in other organizations, like the YMCA, Girl Scouts, etc. Children who are not available for bullying will not be.

- Make sure your child's teacher knows what is going on.

- Encourage your child to seek help from the school staff.

- Volunteer to help supervise school activities.

- Do not ignore your child's reports of being bullied or blame him or her.

- Teach self-respect and respect for others.

- Give your child many positive compliments to increase self-esteem.

- Avoid labeling or name calling, such as calling your child a "sissy."

- Teach your child that while anger is healthy, violence is not.

- Encourage your child to use positive "self-talk."

- Consider driving your child to and from school.

- Do not promise to keep the bullying a secret.

There is no magic solution to making your child bully-proof. Human behavior is unpredictable and complex at times. Some parents blame themselves when their child is bullied; this is understandable, but it is neither accurate nor helpful. The truth is that we do teach others how to treat us by our actions or by our inactions. Instead of blaming themselves for something that is beyond their control, like the actions of bullies and bystanders, it is much more important for parents to teach other children how to treat them. Children can only accomplish this if they learn, at an early age, to create and wear an invisible suit of armor that speaks loudly to would-be bullies, "Don't even think about it." This does not mean that parents should teach their children to be mean and arrogant; this approach has every chance of actually creating a bully. Helping children to use assertiveness skills and to have good self-esteem will, in turn, help them teach other children how to treat them.

"Go placidly amid the noise and haste
and remember what peace there may be in silence.
As far as possible, without surrender
be on good terms with all persons.
Speak your truth quietly and clearly, and listen to others.
Avoid loud and aggressive persons
for they are vexatious to the spirit.
You are a child of the universe, no less than the trees and the stars.
You have a right to be here."

— Excerpt from the "Desiderata," Author Unknown

Parents can effectively teach their child assertiveness skills and self-confidence:

- Allow the child to make some of the decisions in his or her life. Parents, of course, are the shot-callers on the majority of a child's behavior, setting limits, rules, and boundaries. If the child has no interest in taking piano lessons or gymnastics, parents should accept the child's decision. Some things are non–negotiable. Calling your mother an "evil bitch" is not and never will be an option. *Respectfully* explaining to your mother why you are angry with her teaches assertiveness, respect for others, and that expressing feelings is a good thing. If the child can practice this skill at home, he can teach others how to treat him.

- Praise for a child's accomplishment, however small, will reinforce positive, assertive behavior and help build his or her self–esteem. An assertive, confident child is the very last person that a bully wants to try to victimize; they scope out easier targets. The more successes parents praise, the more confidence a child has about being successful in the big, wide world. The assertive child is one who has the confidence to know right from wrong, and strives to do right. This sends a subliminal message to the bully that this child will not play his or her game, nor will this child be a bystander to wrong, unkind behavior.

Parents who raise their children to be kind, helpful, honest, dependable, cheerful, and to hold themselves in high regard but without arrogance will also raise a child who is not afraid to say "no" to a bully, and mean it.

"Being kind doesn't mean we have to be a mat."
– Maya Angelou

Bullying on the School Bus

Yes, it happens here, too. The obvious query is, "Where's the bus driver?" This may be a fair and necessary question. Derek Randel asks his reader to keep in mind that these school district employees are driving a 40-foot vehicle through heavy traffic with a load of other people's children. Bus drivers truly do not have eyes in the back of their heads. Some have been physically attacked, kicked, spat upon, hit, bitten, choked, scratched, and in 2005, a bus driver was shot and killed by a middle school student in Tennessee. Some school districts are placing cameras in school buses; this may or may not prevent bullying on the bus, but it will at least identify the perpetrators unless the camera's view is hidden by the bully's bystanders. The bus drivers are not at fault according to Randel Who emphasizes that many are older men and women who have no business getting involved in a violent incident." This is a controversial stance; parents may well ask why school districts employ bus drivers who are physically unable to intervene in bullying.

In addition to bullying, other types of outrageous misconduct occur on school buses, such as urinating, masturbating, smoking, using drugs, throwing things at passing cars and pedestrians, lap dancing, consensual sex, and rape. Guns and knives are routinely brought onto school buses. While much of the research and literature focuses on bullying in school and during school-sponsored events, little has been written about school bus bullying. Whether this setting for bullying has been either under-reported or under-researched is unknown. Randel (2006) documents a case in Florida where a bus driver reported 79 cases of misbehavior and only one student was suspended as a result. Bus drivers, says Randel, are not likely to bother reporting bullying and other misbehavior when no consequences are administered.

Randel addresses this issue in some detail and offers several solutions:

- Each bus should have two or three adults on board, preferably parent volunteers since hiring bus monitors would be expensive and prohibitive for most school districts. One adult should be at the back of the bus, looking forward. This adult would have a clear, continuous view of the entire bus and could react quickly to inappropriate behavior. Another adult should be available to physically sit next to or between children who are acting inappropriately and/or aggressively. The names of these children should be reported to school officials and documentation submitted detailing the incident. Parents should be contacted and discipline administered at home and school.

• Parents and students should be reminded that riding a school bus is a privilege and a convenience, not a right. Students who habitually misbehave on the bus should be barred from using it. It is then up to the parents to figure out how to get their child to school.

• Since many bullying incidents and other misbehavior occurs while the bus driver is not yet aboard the bus, the driver should instead be first to board the bus to ensure that students are not unsupervised. Victims of bullying are especially vulnerable when the driver is not on the bus.

• Students should wear a picture school ID before they are allowed to board the bus. This serves two purposes: to identify the names of wrongdoers and to prevent non-students from riding the bus with the goal of misbehavior with or to another student.

Bullying on the bus is yet another illustration of the lack of safety of bullied children in places where they should feel safe, i.e. the school bus, school grounds, and at school-sponsored activities. Given the rising number of violent incidents involving schools, what has worked in the past is clearly not working today. Two decades ago, for example, it was unthinkable that a child would bring a loaded weapon onto the bus. Not only was there no reason to do so, since gang violence was still an anomaly in schools, but children feared the wrath of their parents and school personnel. To most adults, it seems literally impossible for a student to be raped on the school bus. Yet, according to Randel, it happens frequently enough to be a statistic. Bullying on the bus, like sexual assaults, seems impossible to adults because they fail to take into consideration the bystanders who see what is happening. Out of fear of the bully or because they are willing eyewitnesses, the other children on the bus shield the bullying from the bus driver's (or the camera's) view.

One of the 12 steps of Alcoholics Anonymous states, "Only a Higher Power can return us to sanity." The founders of AA, Bill W. and Dr. Bob, did not mean that alcoholics are either psychotic or legally insane. They described insanity as doing the same thing repeatedly, and expecting to have different results. If an alcoholic drinks to the black out stage each time he or she drinks, it is insane to expect that this will ever be different unless the alcoholic stops drinking. Applying this concept to bullying on the school bus, if we continue to disregard the personal safety of bullying victims on the bus, it is insane to expect, by some miraculous intervention, that this behavior will change and go into spontaneous remission. School bus bullying will change when parents, teachers, bus drivers, and school district administrators work together to change it.

Dealing Directly with Bullies and their Parents

Things are not always what they seem. John Wayne Gacy, who was convicted and executed for the murders of over 30 young men and boys, was a respected community leader who dressed up as a clown to entertain hospitalized children. He prominently displayed a picture of himself with then First Lady Roslyn Carter. (One cannot help but wonder what she did with that picture.) Sometimes, what we think we know, we do not know at all. We have discussed the need to take bullying very seriously, and we discussed our need to abandon myths and stereotypes about bullies. Parents and teachers must take this concept one step further and engage the bully in a "face off" that clearly communicates to him/her that their number is up: "I know what you've done, I know what you continue to do, and it stops today." Scaglione and Scaglione devised a prototypical plan that involves direct confrontation of the bully and clearly establishing limits and boundaries on his or her behavior, at home and at school. Summarized, this plan involves the following elements:

- Parents, parents, and parents. In another effort to eliminate the bully's support system, the bully's parents should be notified immediately of any bullying activity by their child, and be an active part of the child's rehabilitation.

- A child who is acting aggressively towards other children by bossing them around, yelling at them, or hitting them, should immediately be placed in "time out" to get his/her emotions and actions under control.

- Encourage children to think before they act. Since bullying is sometimes opportunistic, impulse control should be a major focus on the plan.

- Altruistic behavior towards peers should be rewarded in a manner that is meaningful to the child. Positive reinforcement for this type of behavior will help it continue.

- Expose the child to positive role models, preferably other than adult role models. Peer role models can make a distinctive difference in a bullying child's behavior.

- Parents should set and enforce the same limits at home as those enforced at school. The child will learn that what is inappropriate at school is also not appropriate at home.

- Teachers and parents should teach a bullying child the basics of interpersonal social skills, including anger and stress management. Since children learn to bully others because of their lack of social skills, once the bully is provided with opportunities to learn age-appropriate social skills, this will result in an extinction of bullying behavior.

Thus, a crucial part of bully-proofing children is to make noise and lots of it. Instead of perpetuating *omerta*, teachers should discuss this subject openly in classes, such as social studies where human behavior is discussed. Drama clubs can perform skits for the entire grade level on stopping bullies. Physical education classes can help kids work off excess energy that might otherwise be used in bullying. English classes can provide homework on writing essays about why bullying is wrong and what can be done to stop it. Art clubs can create colorful, eye-catching anti-bullying posters and flyers. The possibilities are truly limited only by the imagination.

Bullying at school must be addressed by three sets of adults: the victim's parents, the bully's parents, and teachers and school officials. In the literature, the issue of whether the victim's parents should confront the bully's parents holds different beliefs. Some experts advise parents to avoid the bully's parents and allow school and legal authorities to intervene. As Randel indicated, perhaps the apple did not fall from the tree. Parents should opt for safety of themselves and their child. Referring again to the *Redbook* article by Ellen Welty called "How to Stand Up to a Bully's Mom," Welty advocates victims' mothers directly approaching bullies' mothers. (Since *Redbook* is a magazine for women, fathers do not enter the picture in the article.) Welty recommends seven steps for mothers of victims who choose to intervene by speaking to the bully's mother:

Do not judge her. You do not know anything about their family dynamics and how the bully has been parented.

Propose a private conversation. Discussing this issue is not a talk show, nor should it humiliate the bully's mom. Ask her when the two of you can get together and talk. This is a conversation, not a lecture or an angry tirade.

Ask for her help. Instead of angrily and aggressively confronting her, calmly ask her to be your ally in solving the bullying problem. The best way to gain someone's cooperation is to ask for it, not demand it.

Give just the facts. Describe what you believe has happened between the two children without using the word "bullying." Let her draw her own conclusions about this.

Know what to say if she is receptive. If you get a positive response from the bully's mom, thank her for listening and her promise that she will talk to her child about his/her behavior. Being self-righteous never solves anything, but does make matters worse.

Know what to say if she "stonewalls." You may not receive the type of response you were hoping for. The bully's mom may disbelieve your story or she may dismiss it as "boys will be boys." Hold your ground firmly and assertively; avoid a hostile conclusion to your conversation. Now at least you know what you are dealing with.

Be prepared for a replay. Her child may continue to bully your child. Let her know that nothing has changed, and you would really appreciate her intervening with her child. It might take more than just you to solve this problem.

What if Your Child is the Bully?

Imagine for a moment that you are a loving, responsible parent who has just learned, beyond doubt, that your child has been bullying other children. One parent expressed the moment feeling horrified. How could my child do this? He wasn't raised this way, so where did he learn it? He's been expelled from school. His father won't talk to him, and the tension and shame in our home is unbearable. What am I supposed to do with him? Even his grandparents are ashamed of him.

Barbara Coloroso writes that parents must look honestly and in depth at their child's behavior and whether it has the four markers of bullying: (1) an imbalance of power, (2) intent to harm, (3) threats of further aggression, and (4) terrorizing other children. Coloroso further proposes that terrorizing, intimidating, shunning, tormenting, and ridiculing are not sibling rivalry or peer conflicts. They are acts of bullying. It is important that parents not make light of what happened … that you not try to justify, rationalize, or minimize.

Literature, statistics, and psychobabble aside, this is your *child* – the child you wanted, gave life to, and love dearly. Other children must be bully-proofed to protect themselves from your child. Bystanders do not report or intervene in your child's bullying out of either fear or approval of his or her actions. Without realizing that they are contributing to the bully's actions, parents instinctively look the other way, not wanting to know or suspect that their own child has been terrorizing others. This concept is literally unthinkable.

One of America's most vicious, merciless, and prolific sexual serial killers, Ted Bundy, was a "chameleon" during his youth and early adulthood when he committed, by his own account, rape, murder, and necrophilia upon "three digits" of young women and girls. He hid his true, deviant nature behind a wall of intelligence, wit, and charm. Yet Bundy was a loved child, raised by a mother and stepfather who set limits upon his behavior and rewarded his positive accomplishments. When Bundy stood trial for the rape and murder of twelve-year-old Kimberly Leach in Lake City, Florida, Louise Bundy, his mother, attended every day of his trial in silent love and support, despite the monster that her child became. When Bundy was convicted and sentenced to death, the magnitude of Louise Bundy's deep sorrow – for her son and for his victims and their families – was evident in newspaper photos. While the media dutifully reported the gleeful, chanting crowds ("Burn, Bundy, Burn!") when Bundy was executed, the unimaginable grief of Louise and Johnnie Bundy received no media attention at all. Like Lionel and Joyce Dahmer, the Bundys watched Ted's antics as an innocent child, never imagining the brutal violence he would later perpetrate on his victims and the deviant aberration he would become.

While Ted Bundy and Jeffrey Dahmer are extreme examples of the terror and savagery that one person can inflict upon another, bullies have to begin somewhere. "We're still blaming mothers," Joyce Dahmer once said about the bestial crimes of her son. Without blaming, judging, or criticizing, Barbara Coloroso provides parents with solid information about preventing and recognizing childhood bullying. She advises that, when parents see signs of bullying behavior in their child, they impose discipline upon the child instead of punishment. She differentiates between the two concepts:

Punishment:

- Teaches a child to be aggressive.

- Is degrading and humiliating for the child.

- Denotes blame and pain.

- Does not consider reasons or look for solutions.

- Preempts more constructive ways of relating to the child.

- Deprives the child of the opportunity to understand the consequences of his or her actions, to correct the harm done, or empathize with the bullied victim.

- Deprives the child of feeling ashamed of his/her actions.

Discipline:

- Should be immediate and decisive.

- Is a process that promotes learning; it teaches reconciliation.

- Invites the child to deeply examine his/her own attitudes and behaviors towards others.

- Helps the child develop his/her own moral code.

- Teaches the child to act justly and kindly towards others.

- Teaches the child to control his/her own behavior rather than being controlled.

- Provides the necessary tools to begin the healing and change processes.

- Shows the child exactly what he/she did wrong.

- Gives ownership of the bullying behavior directly to the child who did it.

- Gives the child a process for solving the problem he/she created.

- Leaves the child's dignity intact.

Taking theory into actual practice, Coloroso describes the "three R's" of discipline and how they are used to correct bullying:

Restitution. The child must fix what he or she broke, such as material possessions stolen or destroyed. If the child has caused physical pain to another, an apology must be given. Not a perfunctory "I'm sorry." True repentance for hurting another means assuming responsibility for one's actions, admitting the wrongness of the deed, and expressing a strong desire not to do it again.

In the adult domain, General George S. Patton is a perfect example of the concept of restitution. Gen. Patton may have been one of the most extraordinary military leaders of World War II, but he had a temper and was known to be a narcissistic *"prima donna."* When he publicly slapped and humiliated (bullied?) a soldier experiencing severe combat stress, Gen. Patton was ordered by General Eisenhower, his commanding officer, to publicly apologize to the soldier, to all those who witnessed the incident, and to the entire squadron. Ever obedient to orders, Gen. Patton assumed total responsibility for his actions, admitted that he was wrong, and vowed not to let his temper get out of control in the future. This infamous example of restitution for harming another is exactly what Coloroso describes as an anti-bullying strategy for parents. Whether Gen. Patton was truly repentant for his behavior is between him and his Higher Power.

Resolution. The child must figure out a way to keep bullying from occurring again. Since the bell cannot be un-rung and the harm has already been done, the child must commit to pro-social actions instead of bullying. Children do not want to be "bad." Being pro-social instead of anti-social is much more desirable. Coloroso believes that, if given a choice, children would choose to un-ring that bell if it were possible. Since it is not possible, they can resolve to ring it no further.

Reconciliation. Coloroso describes this as a process of healing with the person one has harmed. It is based upon a child's commitment to honor his/her plan to make restitution and live up to resolutions to bully no more. Children, unlike adults who tend to hold grudges, forgive easily. It is not uncommon for a former bully and a former victim to become friends.

Having real friends, according to Coloroso, is difficult for children who tend towards bullying because this is the only attention they receive from their peers. They mistake bystanders for friends when in reality the bystanders are usually held captive by fear of the bully. Coloroso encourages parents of a bully to teach him or her ten ways to make and keep real friends:

- Show them kindness and respect.

- Stick up for them.

- Be supportive when they need help or advice.

- Tell the truth, but kindly.

- Accept a friend's apology if he or she causes harm.

- Apologize if he or she harms a friend.

- Keep promises to friends.

- Put real effort into friendships.

- Accept friends as they are, without trying to change them.

- Treat others using the "Golden Rule" principle.

"You can't change what you don't acknowledge."
– Dr. Phillip C. McGraw

Derek Randel , with his lengthy history as a teacher, approaches the problem of having a bully in your home a bit differently. First, he writes, parents must know and accept that their child is bullying others. No change can be affected if the problem is not acknowledged. Randel throws down the gauntlet to the bully's parents by asking them to examine and acknowledge what is happening in their own home by answering the following questions.

- Are you a bully at home?

- Do you frequently criticize your child?

- Do you spank or hit?

- Is there an abusive parent in the home?

- Do you yell, use name-calling, or put-downs?

Children, like adults, do what works for them, and what they see working for their parents. If bullying in the home, the school, or the workplace works to give the bully what he or she wants and needs, they will continue to bully, and the victims will continue to allow themselves to be victims. It is disturbing when adult in-home bullies receive reports that their child is bullying others and seek to change the child's actions by more bullying at home.

"Look at yourself instead of looking at me;
Everything that I say and do in your eyes is always wrong
Tell me, where do I belong
In your sick society?
You're no different than me."

— Ozzy Osbourne
"You're No Different"

If there is no difference between the bully's actions in school and the parents' bullying at home, this is an intellectual and emotional "disconnect" for the child. The bully is suspended from school for his/her actions, and is then whipped harshly at home with a belt. The bullying parent is no different than the bullying child. This will never bring anything of value to the bully about his or her actions; confusion, resentment, and anger will be the only result.

"We're just like any other family."
— Tony Soprano

"I'd like to stick this fork in your eye."
— Livia Soprano, Tony's mother

Randel advises parents to look for these signs that their child may be a bully. Bullies become either defensive or aggressive when faced with being held accountable for their actions.

- Does your child use verbal or physical aggression to deal with conflicts?

- Does your child have belongings or money that does not belong to him or her?

- Does your child hang around with other children who appear aggressive?

- Does your child have a difficult time expressing feelings?

- Is your child unable to play cooperative games with other children?

- Does your child become angry when he or she loses a game?

- Have you heard your child talk about "getting even" with others?

- Does your child play inappropriately with younger children?

- Does your child seem to have a strong need to dominate others?

- Is your child oppositional and aggressive towards adults?

- Does your child, at an early age, participate in unlawful activities?

- Is there a lack of supervision at home?

- Does your child minimize his or her wrongdoings by saying, "It was all in fun?"

All these signs demonstrated by one child would be pretty hard to miss unless the parent(s) are also engaging in bullying behavior at home, at work, and in social situations. Some adults – mercifully few – enjoy the "hobby" of dog fighting – pitting one dog against another in a fight to the death. For them, this cruelty is a pleasurable spectator sport. They are unmoved by the suffering of the dogs. In fact, losing dogs are often killed by their owners in disgust. Dog fighting is illegal and carefully concealed by those adults who engage in it. With their own propensity for enjoying cruelty, it is unlikely that these parents would find it to be a problem if told that their child has been bullying other children. Aggression runs rampant in this type of family. Cruelty and violence is the norm; it is not only condoned, it is rewarded. In these cases, attempts by school officials to enlist the aid of parents in eliminating bullying will fall on deaf ears.

For caring and responsible parents who take the conduct of their children seriously, Randel offers the following advice for dealing with a bullying child:

- Always hold children accountable for their actions; accept no rationalizations or excuses.

- Be aware of your tone of voice when talking with your child about his or her bullying; do not lose control.

- Teach your child the art of peaceful negotiation. It is okay to lose; we do not have to win every time.

- Set non-negotiable limits and boundaries and enforce them consistently.

- Make it clear that bullying will not be tolerated, and mean it.

- Teach empathy; ask the child to walk in the footsteps of his or her victim. How would it feel?

- Arrange for effective, non-violent consequences instead of spanking or hitting; try eliminating privileges until the child's behavior changes.

- Forbid violent TV shows or video games; these merely serve as instruction manuals for aggressive bullying.

- Work with schools, not against them. Create a partnership between you and the school.

- Make sure your child knows exactly where you stand on bullying.

- Limit your child's unstructured free time.

- Never keep firearms in your home; at least, none that the child knows about. Unsecured firearms used by your child to commit crimes could result in you being held legally accountable for the child's actions.

God, grant me the serenity to accept the things I cannot change,
Courage to change the things I can,
And wisdom to know the difference.
— St Francis of Assisi

By acknowledging that their child is bullying other children, parents can help the child change. Swift, meaningful discipline, such as that outlined by Coloroso, is an effective approach to ending a child's bullying ways. Since the best predictor of the future is the past, it is expected that childhood bullies will grow up to be demanding, controlling, and intimidating adults. Through their narcissism and selfishness, they stand little, if any, chance of establishing meaningful, healthy, adult relationships with others. They will be difficult co-workers and bosses. They will become well known to divorce court judges. They may have a familiar cell in the county jail. Although the Ted Bundys and Jeffrey Dahmers of the world are thankfully few, America has more than its share of angry, dominating, and despised adult bullies found in the home and the workplace. Unless we, as a society, make childhood bullying a priority, school shootings will continue and perhaps escalate under the "copycat" theory, bullycides will continue, and media violence will continue to saturate young, impressionable minds. This we can change, if we have the courage to do so.

Nathaniel Abraham was eleven years old when he shot and killed eighteen-year-old Ronnie Lee Greene in 1997. At age thirteen, Abraham stood trial as an adult for first-degree murder. When he was arrested for Greene's murder, Abraham had an extensive juvenile record of offenses, such as burglary and assault. He was never called to answer for these crimes, nor did he even know his victim, Greene, who Abraham killed in a random shooting spree. Abraham, the youngest murder defendant in U.S. history, was sentenced as a juvenile and was released from custody on his 21st birthday.

This tragic case serves as an example of a home where limits and boundaries were likely not set, or at the least, not enforced. This is speculation, but if such limits had been set on Abraham's behavior, perhaps this tragedy could have been avoided. Randel describes several types of boundaries that should be nurtured with children:

Physical boundaries — How much intrusion into your personal space will you allow? Bullies almost always violate victim's physical boundaries.

Sexual boundaries — How will you decide how far you are willing to be sexually intimate with someone? Bullies touch others in a sexually inappropriate manner.

Emotional boundaries — How much will you allow others to tell you how to feel? Bullies insist that their bystanders feel "good" about what they are witnessing.

Spiritual boundaries — How much will you allow others to tell you what to believe? Bullies tend to insist on total domination of a victim's thoughts, feelings, and beliefs.

Establishing healthy boundaries with children is essential in preventing them from growing into full-fledged bullies. Many schools of thought about child development indicate that children actually want the healthy adults in their lives to set limits and boundaries because, being children, they are unable to do this for themselves, not because they are *unwilling* but because they are unable. Expecting children to set their own limits and boundaries is akin to expecting a family practice physician to perform brain neurosurgery; the physician may be willing to help the patient, but lacks the skills to perform the procedures. He or she should not be expected to perform what is foreign to them and what is doomed to harm the patient.

So essential are age-appropriate limits and boundaries that Randel points out several undesirable problems that are likely to occur without them:

- Children are more likely to follow their peer group into making unwise choices about sex, drinking, and driving.

- Children do not grow up with the ability or willingness to own their own behavior and its consequences; this leads to a life of unhappiness and turmoil.

- Children allow dominant peers to think, feel, and believe for them instead of making their own choices.

- Weak boundaries make it difficult to tell where the child ends and the dominant peer begins. They have no feelings of "self."

"People who think they know it all seem to know it the loudest."
– Unknown

Bully-proofing our children and taking immediate disciplinary actions when our own child is the bully are two important but incomplete steps in eliminating bullies. As long as the school and community environments inadvertently allow fertile growth of bullying and bystanding, the problem will continue. Dismissing bullying as mere "child's play" could (and probably has) get someone killed; at the least, this thought pattern will result in an emotionally barren adult. Once the issues of bullying and bystanding have received increased awareness, it is time for the school and the community to join forces with parents to finally end this destructive behavior.

chapter eight

Creating Zero Tolerance for School Bullying

Introduction

Manchester, British Columbia, New Zealand, Colorado, Alberta, California, Pennsylvania, Kentucky, Tokyo, Nova Scotia, Virginia, Arkansas.

These are all places where school shootings or bullycides have occurred. To complete the list would fill several pages of this book. Bullying is not an American problem; it is an international problem. Social learning theory proposes that bullying is a learned behavior; as such, it can be un-learned. Better still, it need not be learned at all.

Adults – parents, teachers, school staff, and law enforcement personnel – hold the key to creating a zero tolerance for bullying in schools. Children cannot be expected to accomplish this goal on their own. If they could have done so, they would have. Adults must act, but not over-act. Consider these examples of over-reaction, where zero tolerance became zero common sense:

- Children have been expelled from school because of possession of Midol, Alka Seltzer, cough drops, and mouthwash. Why? Zero tolerance for drugs at school.

- Children have been expelled for wearing Halloween costumes (e.g. pirates, knights, etc.) that included paper swords and obviously toy guns, including light sabers from the Star Wars movies. Why? Zero tolerance for weapons at school.

- A thirteen-year-old was suspended for having a butter knife to cut an apple; she had braces on her teeth. Why? Zero tolerance for weapons at school.

- A first grader was suspended for three days for pointing a breaded chicken finger at a friend like a gun. Why? Zero tolerance for weapons at school.

- Two eight-year-olds were arrested and charged with making terrorist threats for wielding a paper gun in class. Why? Zero tolerance for weapons at school.

- A thirteen-year-old boy was expelled from school for making a list of his enemies and throwing it in the trash, where a teacher found it. Why? Unknown.

- A six-year-old was accused of sexual harassment for running naked out of the bath in his own home to tell the school bus driver to wait for him. Why? Unknown.

A forensic specialist had this to say about these examples: "Are you kidding me?" Randel points out that zero tolerance in schools is a good idea when used properly. However, common sense is sometimes scarce these days. As long as zero tolerance policies continue to be used in unproductive manners, it will lose credibility when the "real thing" occurs, e.g. children bringing guns, knives, box cutters, and other lethal weapons. Schools will cry wolf once too often, and tragedy will be the result.

In this chapter, we will examine school anti-bullying programs that are not over-reactions and that have been proven effective. Bully proofing our schools is difficult and takes very firm commitments by adults and children to make a difference. You will find some helpful forms and projects in the Appendix. We will hear from the experts as well as from parents, teachers, and school administrators. We will look at what works and what does not. This chapter is about action rather than theory.

Olweus's Suggestions at the School Level

Since Dr. Dan Olweus is regarded as the "founding father" of research on bullying, his voice carries much weight with other researchers and writers. His 1993 book *Bullying in School* opened the eyes of the civilized world to the serious problem of school bullying and how it can be stopped. Olweus gives parents and teachers a "whole school" approach, rather than focusing on single episodes. As stated previously, bullying and bystanding flourishes in environments that tolerate its presence. Consider: Bram Stoker designed his frightening character, Count Dracula, with certain flaws and fears. The Count seemed invulnerable, more powerful than any mere mortal. Then, Stoker introduced us to Professor Van Helsing, who knew all the secrets of how to ward off a vampire with crosses, garlic, and flowing water. Better still, the King of the Undead could be vanquished forever by exposure to sunlight and a stake through the heart. Both classic and modern literature present readers with an antagonist who cannot be overcome unless the secret to his or her power is discovered. Even wizard-in-training Harry Potter suggests that the evil wizard (bully?) Voldemort could be destroyed by a *concerted effort* among benign wizards and witches.

So it is with school bullying. Once the light of day is cast upon this practice and the environment that nurtures and allows it to flourish is completely changed, bullying has no place or people to give it power. Without this power, according to the Dracula Theory, bullying will cease to exist.

CASE STUDY: JAMES K.

James is sixteen years old and a resident of a medium-security juvenile institution. His social worker referred him to the mental health clinic because he continually has problems with bullying the other boys in his cottage.

His houseparent responded quickly whenever she observed James' behavior and administered consequences for his actions, such as being confined to his room, having him write sentences like, "Hurting others is wrong," and taking away other privileges, like playing pinball and having dessert. Yet James continued to bully. James stated that he was the oldest of six children of a single mother; he does not know his father. Money was always scarce, and James shoplifted to obtain stylish clothes and sneakers. James was taken into the state's custody as a juvenile delinquent when he seriously assaulted a younger boy at school to steal his New York Yankees windbreaker. James stated that when he assaulted the boy, no one was watching. He was caught when the younger boy explained to his mother why his jacket was missing; the mother called the school principal, and James did not deny the assault or theft. "We have this stupid thing at school, man, about reporting it if somebody hurts you or steals your stuff. The kid was a geek. I didn't think he'd report it because I told him I'd whip his butt if he did. He was supposed to say that he gave the jacket to me. But he had to be a narc about it instead of taking it like a man. That's what I did when something happened to me. The principal, man, what a dork. He rewarded that crybaby for telling, and called the cops on me. Then other little geeks told the principal that I'd done some shit to them and even my mom said she couldn't handle me at home anymore

CASE STUDY: JAMES K.

because I hit my sisters and brothers. Man, I hate those little freaks. And that school sucks. It sucks being here even more and I'm here until I'm eighteen. Man, that's just wrong."

James' story is a product of school intervention against bullying. The children in his school were taught to report bullying, despite threats made by the bully about what would happen to them if they told their story. James was older and larger than his victim, but under the Dracula Theory, the school's anti-bullying environment stopped his actions and made him vulnerable to corrective action. In the group home, his houseparent was not only vigilant about bullying, but she also administered consequences for bullying. Neither of these environments allowed James' bullying to flourish. James expresses his frustration because his number is up; his bullying days are over.

Olweus wrote that the target group in anti-bullying intervention is the entire student population. According to his model, there is no focus on one particular victim or bully. Bully-proofing school measures are aimed at attitudes and conditions that decrease, or change, the school environment to a point where it no longer allows bullying to occur; the law of *omerta* ceases to exist. Olweus describes school interventions that parents and school officials can make that increase their vigilance about bullying and create a force of unity to bullies:

School Conference Day. When a school makes the decision to become a bully-free environment, a conference day allows the principal, teachers, the school counselor, and the school nurse, along with selected parents and students, to arrive at an overall, long-term plan for the school in becoming an anathema for bullying behavior. This creates a cohesive group that is vigilant and intolerant of bullying.

Supervision and Outdoor Environments. Although bullying does occur on the victim's way to and from school, the majority of this behavior occurs in school. When students are at lunch, during recess, and in school activities, adults must actively monitor what is happening in this environment rather than simply being present. In addition to being there, adults must be prepared to act swiftly and decisively if they observe bullying and bystanding. It is better to intervene too quickly than not quickly enough. The requisite attitude in this scenario is that "we will not accept bullying" from both the students and the adults.

Contact Telephone. Olweus suggests that, if bullying victims are reluctant to engage in face-to-face reporting, they can call a certain telephone number anonymously and tell the school counselor or a teacher volunteer what is happening to them. Armed with the knowledge that bullying is occurring in the school, these adults can take measures against bullying that benefit the entire school. The victim(s) need never actually come forward if they fear retaliation. This is similar to a "whistle blowing" action by an adult that sees and reports wrongdoing on a corporate or governmental level.

A General PTA Meeting. Olweus suggests that this is an excellent way for parents and teachers to form a united stand against bullying. If these adults are acting in concert, it is impossible for the bully to create a split between parents and teachers.

Teacher Groups for Developing a Social Milieu of the School. Instead of frenzied bursts of concern and actions by teachers against bullying, Olweus recommends *constant readiness* to identify and act on bullying. Each teacher must become an active, but steady and calm, member of the school's overall social milieu. Teachers should meet at least weekly to discuss bullying incidents, how they were addressed, and further plans to create a school environment that does not inadvertently foster bullying. Olweus describes these meetings as *collegial support groups* that promote a common ground among teachers against school bullying, as well as common solutions. Under the Dracula Theory, such an approach among teachers is the bully's worst nightmare: a united group that exposes their secret activities, once protected by *omerta*, to the light of zero tolerance.

Study Groups in Parent-Teacher Associations. Olweus advises that when both parents and teachers educate themselves on school environments that inadvertently foster bullying, the probability of creating a zero tolerance environment is greatly increased. Study of the literature on school bullying and inviting expert guest speakers to increase their knowledge base about bullying creates not only zero tolerance for bullying but also provides further information about creating a non-bullying school environment.

A British Model to Prevent Bullying

It is fair to say that since Olweus published his research findings and recommendations in 1993, other researchers have taken up the cause. George Varnava (2002) wrote in his book, *How to Stop Bullying in Your School*, "Children have the right to be educated in a safe environment and every member of the school community is equally entitled to that right. Bullying is an infringement of that entitlement." Varnava outlines eight stages in an anti-bullying strategy for schools in the United Kingdom:

	ANTI-BULLYING STRATEGY FOR SCHOOLS
1	A whole-school action plan with all sectors of the school community represented in the plan.
2	Establishing a commitment: "We aim to be a bullying-free school."
3	The commitment is publicized internally and externally, providing a basis for collaboration with parents and the local community.
4	A practical anti-bullying program is introduced in the school.
5	Self-auditing helps schools determine if their program is working.
6	Action is taken to address specific risk areas.
7	A whole-school review of the anti-bullying process is undertaken.
8	Each school formulates its own criteria for evaluating their progress and reducing bullying.

Although Varnava researched and wrote about school bullying in the United Kingdom, his findings and intervention plans are relevant for American society as well. Violence, he believes, , "is epidemic in British society and most of us fear it. It permeates our lives, our culture and our language." Varnava, a meticulous researcher, cites film and television listings during the Christmas season of 2002:

- *Killer Contract*

- *Mortal Combat 2*

- *Recipe for Revenge*

- *Suburban Commando*

- *Shoot to Thrill*

- *The Long Kill*

- *Clubbed to Death*

- *Merchant of Death*

- *Toy Soldiers*

- *Stick Fighting Warriors*

- *Blood on Her Hands*

How many more such offerings could Americans add, e.g. *Kill Bill, Bum Fights, Natural Born Killers, Reservoir Dogs, Scarface, Pulp Fiction, Nightmare on Elm Street, The Sopranos, Deadwood, Saw, Friday the 13th , Halloween, Fight Club, The Godfather series*, and *Gladiator*. Even *The Passion of the Christ*, despite its redeeming social value, is an extremely violent movie. Director Mel Gibson's goal was for people to understand the truth about the agony of Jesus Christ as he was executed, and that crucifixion was an atrocity committed regularly by Roman rulers. Okay, we get it. We are adults. Maybe children, though, cannot get it because they have not lived long enough to understand what Gibson is showing them on the screen. Varnava calls violence by children "a product of neglect" and writes that, "Children don't invent anti-social behavior. They learn quickly, are easily influenced and they understandably react to any of the many forms of neglect they may suffer." One is given to wonder, due to their saturation of media violence, how much school bullying has been perpetuated by children who want to imitate violent media figures.

To address violence in schools, including bullying, Varnava

developed a "Checkpoint for Schools," with the goal of working towards a non-violent society and reducing the number of school confrontations. The Checkpoints consist of a framework that represents the main aspects and dimensions of school life:

- Home/School/Community

- Values

- Organization

- Environment

- Curriculum

- Training

The Checkpoints are similar to the peer review process; they are used to determine "how are we doing?" as far as creating a non-violent, bullying-free school environment. There is an adult version of the Checkpoints, as well as a "kid-friendly" version with simpler language. *Towards a Non-Violent Society – Checkpoints for Young People* (Varnava 2000) is a companion to *Checkpoints for Schools* (Varnava 2000). This booklet for school-age children provides some facts to help students understand the seriousness of its contents:

- Violence hurts; it can hurt your body and your feelings.

- People do not have to be violent; they learn to be violent, usually as a child.

- Up to 60 percent of young people are bullied at some point during their lifetime.

- Most children at home are smacked.

- In 90 percent of cases when there is violence between adults at home, children see and hear it.

Finally, Varnava makes the point that, children are not natural bullies or instinctively violent. Many bullies use violence as a means of establishing their place in the pecking order of society, masking their own vulnerability with their dominating tactics. Bullying in schools is damaging to people and institutions alike. Schools do not teach misbehavior, they are not the cause of truancy, they do not encourage bullying or condone criminality. It is unjust when they are blamed for any of these. This is a very telling statement; since Varnava exonerates both the bullying child and the schools from any culpability, and in an earlier statement refers to violence as a "product of neglect," it is clear that he is pointing the finger of blame directly at the bully's parents. He proposes that in dealing with bullying, schools are able to present alternatives to violence and counteract the many damaging influences to which children are subjected.

By Varnava's reasoning, we should excuse children who bully because their parents have loud, sometimes physical arguments. We should excuse bullies who have been allowed exposure to media violence. If a child's parent(s) commits a crime, and the child subsequently engages in bullying, we should excuse him or her from accountability. By these standards, it is probably not too far off the mark to suggest that the great majority of American school children who are bullied are in serious trouble; their tormentors will never be called upon to account for, or correct, their actions. The flaw in Varnava's thinking is that millions of American and British citizens grew up in homes where their parents were loud and sometimes abusive, they were allowed to watch media violence, and had an incarcerated parent. Yet these individuals never engaged in bullying as children or aggressive violence as adults.

Varnava does, rather briefly, explain that children who bully others must be held accountable. However, he implies that the school must do this because parents do not: "Schools have to make a stand on discipline, *particularly when it seems that everyone else has given up* [emphasis ours]. The disciplinary principle that most apply is that when an individual cannot or will not conform to the requirements of the school community, then he or she no longer deserves a place there. This is harsh punishment for a child but it is an effective sanction. In the practice of many schools, a clear distinction is made between punishment and correction. If the fault can be corrected, punishment is unnecessary. There is room for flexibility in dealing with individuals but no room for ambiguity." It could be argued that shunning a child for bullying is not the answer. In fact, social isolation only compounds the problem.

To bully-proof a school, Varnava focuses on the need for anti-bullying training for school staff and children. In his model, parents are excluded from this training. In his outline for staff training, Varnava discusses the need for pleasant introductions, keeping a sense of humor, avoiding the staff room for training, giving attention to light, heating, comfort, and good visual effects, such as flowers in the room. A catered lunch should be held in a different room. Teachers are encouraged to remember the "wise teacher's rule: never get between the children and their food." In his entire outline for staff training, Varnava uses the word "bullying" only one time.

In his model for training school students about anti-bullying, Varnava appears to recommend that the students train themselves. Curiously, he makes no mention of adult guidance in the training. However, Varnava cites the importance of sound, positive relationships among students as being an effective tool in learning pro-social interpersonal skills. Teachers have a daily opportunity to guide these positive relationships.

Varnava finds suitable for discussion and debate among students and staff the following verbatim topics that were initiated from newspaper headlines in the UK:

- Life of violence can be predicted at age three.

- School's violence culture condemned.

- Swat squad of teachers sent to tame school from hell.

- More young children watching TV violence after 9 p.m.

- Offer help, not expulsion.

- Germany attacks Britain's use of child soldiers.

- Security in playtime patrols.

- Staff underestimate how much they can improve behavior.

- Bullying rife in Britain's caring jobs.

- Martial arts therapy for troubled teenagers.

- Exclusion promotes bad behavior.

- Truancy drive on the buses.

In his book, Varnava's final sentence, "There will be no bullying," describes his Nirvana-like vision of schools in the future. What help his book offers in accomplishing this goal must be left to the reader.

CASE STUDY: MAX W.

Max is a 36-year-old Caucasian male, married with two children. He has a younger brother, Alex, age 33. Alex and Max grew up in an intact home with their mother and father. Max is not a mental health patient; neither he nor Alex has any mental health history. Both have college degrees and have secure employment. According to Max, he and Alex have happy, successful marriages and good relationships with their children.

Almost a year ago, Max decided that he wanted to record, in writing, his childhood history hoping that it would unburden him of some anger and resentment he felt towards his father. In correspondence with this author, Max related that he grew up being physically and emotionally abused by his father. Max wrote that his father held a series of high-risk jobs, primarily as a fire fighter. He held his children to rigorous and, according to Max, unrealistic standards of perfection.

The boys were expected to make outstanding grades and excel at all sports activities in school. Any performance that did not meet his father's expectations was punished by severe physical punishment. Max wrote that his father also physically abused their mother, especially if she tried to intervene for Max and Alex's safety. Max's father called the boys names like "sissy," "crybaby," "bed wetter," "queer," "girly-girl," "punk," and "dumb ass."

If Max cried when his father was beating him, he would be beaten worse. Max described an incident when he was around seven years old and had done something that displeased his father. Max wrote that his father picked him up and slammed him into the wall several times. Max was so frightened that he urinated in his pants. This enraged his father even further, and he beat Max into unconsciousness. . Max wrote that his father's control over the family was absolute. He told Max and Alex what classes to take and what sports to participate in. He insisted on knowing the exact whereabouts of the boys and their

CASE STUDY: MAX W.

mother, and told them when they must be home. Any deviation from their father's rules resulted in a beating.

Max's maternal and paternal grandparents knew about the abuse but did not intervene. Max and Alex told no one out of fear of retaliation from their father. When they were both old enough, Max and Alex left home and worked their way through college. Max has no history of domestic violence, no history of substance abuse, has never committed a crime, and believes he is happy and emotionally stable. His mother died ten years ago.

Last year, Max contacted his father by telephone for the first time in almost 20 years; he hoped for reconciliation with his father and wanted to gain some closure regarding his childhood abuse. Max stated that his father did not seem glad to hear from him after all those years. "It was like talking to a stranger," Max wrote, "since he virtually was by that time." After a very brief conversation, Max's father told him he had to hang up because he had to go somewhere. Neither father nor son has initiated further contact. "He hasn't changed," Max wrote. "I don't know what I expected. At least now I know that there's no hope. He doesn't even know the names of his grandchildren. That's my Dad."

"There are more pleasant things to do than beat up people."
– Muhammad Ali

An Early Bullying Intervention Model

In their well-received book *The Bullying Prevention Handbook* (1996), John Hoover and Ronald Oliver presented a school bullying intervention model that even a decade later has relevance in today's schools, homes, and communities. They wrote that little excuse, remains for not preventing and treating bullying in American schools. The school must protect the students' right to be safe while growing, learning and developing. Hoover and Oliver describe the primary elements of this intervention model as necessary precursors of a physically and emotionally safe school. They list these underpinnings of an anti-bullying school:

- **Bullying is unacceptable** — Based upon Olweus's 1993 findings that good intentions do not solve bullying problems, parents, school officials, and students must set and enforce behavioral standards, with zero tolerance for bullying. Even when bullying awareness was in its infancy, Hoover and Oliver recognized that bullying is not just comprised of physical abuse. They wrote that schools should have "speech codes" that address verbal bullying, such as taunting, name-calling, and threatening. Public humiliation of students in any form is strictly prohibited.

- **The Empathetic School** — Students must accept the concept that they are their brother's keeper and must deal ethically with other students, particularly those who are most vulnerable to being bullied. Although Hoover and Oliver published their book years before the role of the bystander was clearly defined and understood, they appear to suggest that other students must be bystanders for good rather than for cruelty. Students should be taught about interdependence, not social isolation, and the worth of each individual. Some researchers found that bullies do not tolerate cultural, racial, or religious differences well (Coloroso, 2003, McGrath, 2007). In an empathetic school, diversity is celebrated rather than condemned.

- **The Anti-Bullying Information Campaign** — Hoover and Oliver note that getting the anti-bullying message out was a central feature of Dr. Dan Olweus's 1991 campaign for the Norwegian Ministry of Education. In 2000, Kohut asked: How do you make roaches scatter and run? You turn the light on them. The rule of *omerta* should be extinguished.

• **Referral Mechanisms** — Some students, bullies as well as victims, should be brought to the attention of helping professionals inside and outside the school. For these mechanisms to function properly, the school must develop a climate that encourages students to admit that they have been harmed, have faith that with this admission, they will be taken seriously, and receive help.

• **Group and Individual Psychotherapy** — The earliest known method for working with bullies and victims is the Common Concern Method proposed by Pikas in 1989. It is designed to lessen the pathological impact of bullying on school-age children. This method helps bullies to understand the feelings of their victims and helps all those involved reach a solution. This is a form of cognitive retraining; the bully learns to change his or her thought patterns about bullying and about the victim(s). Similar in structure to Albert Ellis's Cognitive Behavioral Therapy, the Common Concern Method advocates that if one changes his or her thoughts (cognitions), he or she can change feelings and behavior. The Pikas approach worked in the early 1990s, and it works now with equal efficacy.

• **Family-Based Approaches** — In their early intervention model, Hoover and Oliver characterized a bully's family as being loosely structured with a cold emotional climate and a lack of supervision. This hostile environment fostered aggression and bullying. In contrast, they wrote, families of victims appear to be over-involved and highly protective. Today, more than a decade later, some researchers would challenge these views as being inaccurate stereotypes. However, it has long been agreed that to deal effectively with bullying, a program must address family dynamics of both bullies and victims.

- **Bibliotherapy and Coping Strategies** — Hoover and Oliver note that many fiction writers broach the subject of bullying. Teachers can use such literature to introduce the topic of bullying and initiate discussion on the subject, including possible solutions. For example, the best-selling author in American history, Stephen King, often includes bullying in his plot lines; it seems that King loves to see the "bad guys" get the comeuppance they deserve. This theme can be found in *The Stand*, *Salem's Lot*, *Bag of Bones*, *Dreamcatcher*, *Needful Things*, *Carrie*, *It*, *The Green Mile*, and one of King's novelettes, *The Body*, which was made into a movie entitled *Stand by Me* and starred Will Wheaton, River Phoenix, Corey Feldman, and Keifer Sutherland. Before he began his TV career as hero Jack Bauer in *24*, Sutherland and his bystanders terrorized small-town kids Wheaton, Feldman, and Phoenix through threats, intimidation, and general nastiness. One of the most satisfying moments in the book and movie occurred when Wheaton found himself in a face-off with Sutherland, aided by a loaded and cocked pistol. Sutherland was forced to back away from the children with a vow to get even. But in a Stephen King story, the bad guys and bullies never triumph, not even the Devil himself in *The Stand*. Teachers and parents, of course, should not recommend that victims of bullying confront their tormentor with a loaded pistol, and King's books are not suitable in content or language for children. However, there are King-like books and stories, including the Harry Potter series, suitable for children that teach the concept that "wrong" does not triumph when individual and group valor prevails. Hollywood often teaches children that the bad guys can, if they choose, become good guys. Evil Darth Vader returned to his roots as kindly and courageous Anakin Skywalker. The Terminator, who still resembled Arnold Schwarzenegger, became a benevolent savior of humankind. Captain Jack Sparrow, of the *Pirates of the Caribbean* trilogy, is a scoundrel with the heart of a hero. These messages are not lost on children; books and movies convey the idea that bullies can not only be defeated, they can change their attitudes and behavior as well.

- **Referrals to Mental Health Agencies** — Hoover and Oliver note that in any school there are severely troubled children, especially those who are abused at home and/or have serious mental health problems. Schools should have a well-established, working system for identifying these children and referring them to mental health and special education authorities. Although Hoover and Oliver fail to mention it, it is also essential that school staff report any suspicions of child abuse by parents or caretakers to the local child protection agency. School staff are legally "mandated reporters," meaning that by law, they *must* report any suspicion of child abuse and/or neglect. There is no wiggle-room in the law. School staff do not have to *know* that a child is being abused or neglected at home; they must report even suspicions. Their failure to abide by this law, enacted in every state in the nation, will cost them their jobs and, with teachers, their license to teach. Most important, failure to report suspicions of child abuse and neglect can result in the death of the child. Mental health practitioners are also mandated reporters and are held to these same legal standards.

School, Community, and Home Education About Bullying

Dr. P.C. McGraw wrote, "You can't change what you don't acknowledge." Taking this concept one step further, you also cannot change something you know nothing about. Schools, communities, and parents know that bullying exists (in the vernacular, a "no brainer"). However, knowing something exists and knowing what to do about it are at opposite ends of the knowledge spectrum. Without exception, the major researchers who examined the phenomenon of bullying (Olweus, Varnava, Coloroso, Scaglione and Scaglione, McGrath, Randel, Hoover and Oliver, to name but a few) indicate that before bullying can be stopped, all the adults who are change agents must know as much as possible about bullies, victims, and bystanders.

In 1996, Hoover and Oliver describe the basics of an information campaign about bullying:

> *Someone must take the initiative to acknowledge and shout about the hippo in the living room. An information campaign must have a hero: a teacher, a coach, a parent, a principal, a school counselor — even a student.*

> *The movie* Network *contains a memorable scene where an eccentric*

newsman with a desire for social change encouraged everyone watching to go to his or her open window and shout into the street, "I'm as mad as hell, and I'm not going to take this anymore!" And the people did just that. Imagine what would happen if bullied children shouted at the top of their lungs, "I'm being bullied, and I'm not going to take it anymore!" The hippo in the living room must be acknowledged, the law of omerta must be broken, and a solid information base must be gathered and disseminated. Those affected by bullying need to become mad as hell, and refuse to take it anymore.

One visionary hero turns into two heroes. Then three and four. As the information campaign gains momentum, a bullying prevention committee forms. Hoover and Oliver recommend that this committee contain representatives of those who are negatively affected by bullying, i.e. parents, teachers, administrators, community members, such as representatives from the PTA and the school board. The committee must include members of the student body of all ages and grades. The school principal is an essential member of the committee. His or her leadership and endorsement of an anti-bullying campaign lends credibility and power to the tasks ahead, especially in matters of discipline and zero tolerance for bullying.

The committee should gain and widely disseminate information about bullying. Some adults actively resist anti-bullying campaigns. They hesitate to shine the light on bullying because of the controversy it may create; some individuals do not do well with conflict and adopt a "peace at any price" attitude. Some parents resist having their job as parents usurped by the school. Others view bully-busting as a hopeless, unattainable goal. Finally, some adults may believe that bullying is a natural part of the childhood social order. Providing real, practical information about bullying may help convince these parents of their thinking errors or such information will make no *headway in recruiting these parents as allies. They may even say that what their child does is no one else's business. Either they get it or they do not. Bullying is everyone's business*

Every single individual affected by bullying should take a stand against it in a global affirmation that they are not going to take it anymore. A button distributed to Norwegian children after Olweus's all-out campaign against bullying read, "Friends do not bully friends." In an information campaign, imagine how many slogans students and involved adults could come up with: "Bullying is wrong." "I will report bullying." "Our school is a bully-free place to learn." "Zero tolerance for bullying." To show solidarity and support for students, the principal, teachers, and parents should use the media to their best advantage by carrying anti-bullying knowledge campaigns to the newspaper, local radio, and local television. This strategy is frequently used in anti-drug campaigns. Once, drug addiction was a secret that no one talked about. Now, celebrities by the score, ministers, teachers, politicians, writers, and many others have made their addiction(s) known to the public, along with their promise of rehabilitation. There is no reason why the same approach could not be used with bullying. Hoover and Oliver recommend public or town meetings, printed educational materials about bullying for adults and children, posters in and around the school drawn by children, and letters sent to the parents of every child enrolled in a school explaining the anti-bullying education campaign and the school's stance on bullying. Hoover and Oliver also recommend in-class activities, like watching videotapes and listening to popular music that contain anti-bullying messages. Class role playing exercises allow every student to gain a better understanding of bullying by portraying the bully, the victim, or the bystander. Children who have a way with words can help an information campaign by writing prose or poetry about bullying from any point of view they choose.

It is interesting to speculate how bullies in school might react to a community-wide information and education campaign designed to eliminate bullying. Teachers and staff may not know all the bullies in a particular school, but they are well-known by the students. Since bullies rely on intimidating their victims and bystanders into remaining silent about their bullying, one can reasonably speculate, based on the research, about how they might respond to massive cooperative efforts to eliminate the acts that are, by now, an ingrained part of their attitudes and behaviors:

- Stop all bullying immediately.

- Vehemently deny that they ever bullied another child.

- Up the ante by seriously threatening harm to any victim or bystander that names him or her as a bully.

- Carry out those threats if necessary.

- Adopt a manipulative pro-social attitude and "repent" of their past bullying, vowing to cease all such behavior.

- Have a genuine "ah ha!" epiphany that what he or she has been doing to other children is wrong and taking sincere advantage of this opportunity for change.

It is recommended that escalated bullying carry severe consequences, and that genuine desires to change be applauded and encouraged, bringing about reconciliation between bullies and their former victim(s). To relinquish the behavior that was their source of power and control, bullies will initially be suspicious and fearful; if they do this, then they will be vulnerable. Luke Skywalker without his light saber, Superman weakened if Lex Luthor throws a block of Kryptonite at him, Dirty Harry without his .44 magnum handgun. To successfully bring about genuine change takes a heroic action by the former bully and should be noticed and rewarded.

"We're second-chance people. I was given a second chance. Where mercy is shown, mercy is given."
— Dwayne "Dog" Chapman, fugitive recovery agent

Creating Caring in Schools

CASE STUDY: JUAN D.

"I was raised in New York City. The place is huge. Going to school there was like spending your days in a city of its own. The teachers didn't know our names most of the time. So we had to wear name tags, and kids used to put all kinds of phony names on them like Marilyn Monroe, Errol Flynn, Tina Turner, Ringo Starr, and shit like that. My name was Bruce Springsteen, and nobody even noticed.

When I was in the eighth grade, some guy whose nametag said "Steven Tyler" (lead singer of the rock band Aerosmith) started hassling me. I didn't know who he was or anything about him like what grade he was in. He didn't know me, either. I guess I just had one of those faces. I never did find out why he picked on me. Anyway, this guy used to wait outside my science classroom just so he could thwack me upside the back of my head and knock my books around. I started carrying my books in a book bag. Didn't help. He just yanked off my book bag and drop-kicked it down the hallway. Everybody laughed while I ran to get it, and they kicked it further away. Other guys called it "Springsteen hallway soccer." There was never a teacher anywhere around.

CASE STUDY: JUAN D.

This went on my entire eighth grade year. "Stephen and Bruce" became celebrities. I tried to laugh it off, but it really did bug me, man. Nobody spoke up for me because nobody knew me. Friends are something you don't have if you go to public school in New York City. Your friends were back in the neighborhood. I never told any adults about Stephen. They didn't know me and they didn't know him. What were they gonna do? Stay beside me every minute? You can't force people to care about you. I didn't tell my parents because we're Mexican, and my Dad would have just told me to act like a man and beat his ass. I was just a kid, man. How was I supposed to kick anybody's ass?

By the end of that school year, I made up my mind that I wasn't going back there no matter what. And I didn't.

I spent the summer learning to paint houses with my Dad, and he didn't care if I went to school or not since he didn't graduate either. The thing that bothered me the most was that in that school nobody gave a crap about me or even knew my name. Now I keep to myself a lot. That's the way I learned to be. If anybody notices you, you get hassled. If you stay out of the way, you don't. You're just invisible. There's nothing wrong with me, mentally. I just want to be left alone. Why can't I do that? Why does that bug people and make them think I'm mental?"

Juan's story illustrates the feelings of invisibility that some children feel in school, especially when they feel isolated from adults and peers alike. He paints a bleak picture of a huge school with no atmosphere of caring about individual students. Bullying can, and does, proliferate in this type of setting. It often goes unreported because students feel this lack of caring exists not because school staff are cold-hearted but because students outnumber them in excess of 30 to one. With children bringing guns and knives to school on a regular basis in large cities, a situation like Juan's would be of low priority since no one was physically hurt, no weapons were brandished, and there were no complaints of inaction by Juan's parents.

Barbara Coloroso discusses the type of caring school environment needed to be effective against bullying. Schools should have:

- A strong, positive statement of the school's policy of zero tolerance for bullying.

- A succinct definition of bullying, with examples.

- A declaration of the right of individuals and groups in the school – students, teachers, other workers, and parents – to be free of victimization by others.

- A statement of the responsibility of those who witness peer victimization to seek to stop it.

- Encouragement of students and parents with concerns about victimization to speak with school personnel about their concerns.

- A comprehensive description of how the school proposes to deal with the bully/victim problem.

- A plan to evaluate their policy in the near future.

Coloroso is a strong proponent of Dr. Dan Olweus's recommendations for creating a caring, bully-free school environment. She cites the acclaimed Steps to Respect program that is based on Olweus's work in this field. The program is in use in U.S. and Canadian elementary schools with good results. It has the goal of not only creating a caring, zero tolerance school setting, but it also teaches children the basics of healthy, supportive, and empathetic interpersonal relationships. Bullying is incompatible with these types of relationships, and children learn to recognize, refuse, and report bullying to adults. Steps to Respect is one of the few programs that addresses the role of the bystander; it emphasizes that all children are responsible for eliminating bullying in their school.

Steps to Respect recommends that information about bullying in school be obtained directly from the students of that school via anonymous reports. If we want to know what is going on with children, we must ask children. As long as children have no fear of retaliation, they are notoriously honest, as if they have been waiting to be asked, to spill forth information they have been holding inside for personal safety reasons but that they badly want to tell.

Even though they rebel against them at times, children want to know what the rules are and how they will be enforced. Schools need to create strong social norms against bullying, along with programs to prevent, identify, and cope with bullying. Bullied children must know that they will be believed, supported, and protected, with adults taking responsibility for the safety of all students. They want to be taken seriously. Children feel safest when a continuing adult presence prevents overt bullying. In classrooms, hallways, the cafeteria, the library, and on the school bus, the presence of vigilant adults vastly increases safety. Children themselves are rarely able to stop bullying unless, like Will Wheaton in *Stand by Me*, they happen to have a loaded pistol handy. As amusing as this scene may have been on the movie screen, its humor fades with the knowledge that *this really does happen*. Only in real life, the angry, weary victim pulls the trigger, and the body count is real. "You can't make people care about you," Juan stated in the previous case study. But schools can unequivocally prohibit bullying behavior in school. Unless responsible adults ensure safety and teach children to treat each other with respect and support, death will continue to stalk the hallways of our schools.

The Supreme Court Speaks

Researcher, author, and human relations attorney Mary Jo McGrath recounts the landmark case of *Oncale vs. Sundowner* (USSC 1998) where the U.S. Supreme Court found that same-sex harassment was illegal discrimination under Title VII and Title IX. Justice Scalia, writing the unanimous opinion of the Court, stated, "The real social impact of workplace or school-related behavior often depends upon a constellation of surrounding circumstances, expectations and relationships which are not fully captured by a simple recitation of the words used or the physical acts performed. Common sense and an appropriate sensitivity to social context will enable courts and juries to distinguish between simple teasing and rough-housing among members of the same sex, and conduct which a reasonable person in the complaining person's position would find severely hostile or abusive."

In everyday terms, the Supreme Court, by a unanimous decision, came one step closer to finding that bullying among boys and among girls is legally actionable. The Court draws a line between teasing and hostile, abusive behavior. In 1998, the Supreme Court used the term "harassment" to describe this conduct. It is likely that almost a decade later, the Court will hear and decide cases of bullying, using this word to define the actionable behavior involved, regardless of the age of the complainant.

Six Hours a Day

Scaglione and Scaglione make the point that children spend about six hours a day during the school term interacting with other children. On the average, this is more time than they spend interacting with adults at home. Therefore, it seems reasonable and prudent that all schools have an effective program to prevent bullying on school grounds and at school-sponsored activities. Research indicates, that where schools have a complacent attitude towards bullying, burying their heads and looking the other way and not enforcing rules against it, bullying becomes part of the landscape." Six hours a day, five days a week, is a long time to spend being physically and emotionally tormented. By doing the math and taking into consideration the amount of time that children spend at school, Scaglione and Scaglione describe the ideal environment for a caring, bully-proof school:

Warm and accepting. In such a school, the feeling of "community" becomes obvious to others visiting the school. There is much involvement among staff, students, and parents. Adults lead by example, not by threats of punishment. They demonstrate kindness, empathy, and encouragement. Teachers seek out the positive in students, rewarding and praising accomplishments. They also reward pro-social interactions among the students. Character education is just as much a part of the curriculum as reading or science; children learn what it means to be respectful, honest, kind, and caring towards others, other children, and adults alike. In addition to correcting inappropriate behavior, teachers go out of their way to catch students doing something right, and rewarding that behavior. Students learn to accept and tolerate differences in each other; others are not excluded because they are different.

Clear Expectations and Consistent Enforcement of the Rules.
Teachers set clear expectations of acceptable behavior. Children are
expected to help others who may be picked on or excluded. Failure
to intervene in bullying is just as unacceptable as actual bullying;
there are no innocent bystanders. Consequences for breaking
rules are fully explained and equally, consistently enforced. The
principal is a frequent visitor to classrooms, indicating his or
her endorsement and involvement of anti-bullying campaigns.
If bullying occurs, the principal swiftly intervenes and contacts
the child's parents. No incident of bullying, however small, goes
unaddressed by responsible adults.

**Educates Everyone on How to Get Along and How to Stop
Bullies.** Beginning in kindergarten, children are taught social
skills and problem solving. Kindness, altruism, and selflessness
are emphasized. As children grow older, age-appropriate
bibliotherapy and movie therapy are used to help children
differentiate between pro-social and anti-social behavior.
Children are taught Alfred Adler's concept of "social interest."
They build empathy skills and how to respond to bullying safely
but decisively. The school creates a climate that fosters reporting
of bullying.

Lovely indeed these nirvana-like schools sound, but are they
realistic in today's world where teachers often have more than
30 students in one class? Derek Randel (2006) has more than
87 recommendations on how to create an anti-bullying school
environment, far too many to include here. Perhaps teachers and
other school staff are reading this book, thinking, "There's no
way I can do all this. I'm lucky just to get through today's English
lesson." Theory is usually like that: It sounds wonderful, well-
meaning, and effective when we read about it, but putting it into
practice is extremely time consuming and complex. If a theoretical

program is not "do-able" except in a perfect universe, it is useless and creates self-blame by parents, teachers, community members, and students when they are unable to implement a theoretical program. This does not mean that all schools should not have some type of anti-bullying campaign and is not meant to divest adults of their responsibility to create a bully-free environment. It simply means that doing *something* is a heck of a lot better than feeling overwhelmed and doing *nothing*.

"The better we feel about ourselves, the fewer times we have to knock someone down in order to feel tall."
— Odetta

Program Evaluation

Once a school has established and maintained an anti-bullying program, whether it is successful or not, it must be evaluated. Each time a school shooting, bullycide, homicide, or beating occurs, all over the nation school superintendents, principals, and school boards scurry to make sure they can report to their community, their lawmakers, and Larry King that their school is completely bully-proof because they have an effective anti-bullying campaign in place. They proudly announce, "It can't happen here. Not in our school." Although McGrath exposed this myth for the wishful thinking that it is, a community needs to feel soothed and confident that parents can safely send their children to school, and at the end of the day, they will not come home in a body bag. Parents tend to accept what they are told about the structure and effectiveness of the school's bully-proof environment because this is what they want to hear, what they want to believe. All too often, no one pays any attention to that man behind the curtain who is creating an illusion with smoke and mirrors. Oz, the Great and Powerful, exists because parents *want* him to exist.

To develop the most effective anti-bullying environment that involves both prevention and treatment, schools must reflect upon whether or not their program works. This means that they need to collect data from the only people who can truly answer their question — the students. In their anti-bullying model, Hoover and Oliver suggest that data should be collected in the fall, midyear, and spring. This time frame appears to ask the students, "How are we doing?" as far as bullying prevention and intervention. Being anonymous, and with a meaningful "flip," students can give the school a report card about how its anti-bullying campaign is, or is not, working for them. School officials in Texas middle schools had a rude awakening in March 2006, when these surveys indicated that principals and students have very different definitions of bullying. The majority of principals surveyed considered their school to be safe, and believe school procedures and policies were effective in reducing bullying. However, researchers discovered that students in those same schools rarely considered their schools to be safe, and felt that administrators did far too little to stop bullying (*The Montana Standard*, December 4, 2006).

To have an effective program, there has to be data. To have data, there have to be questions. Hoover and Oliver suggest that schools collect data on bullying with these goals in mind:

- Is the program successful in decreasing bullying or its impact on students?

- How much was bullying decreased?

- Which specific bullying behaviors were reduced?

- Were students aware of anti-bullying efforts?

- Did students value the activities that were organized around the theme of anti-bullying?

To collect data, there has to be tools and instruments. In *The Bullying Prevention Handbook*, Hoover and Oliver include questionnaires and suggested interview questions that they have placed in the public domain to be used and reproduced at will. To summarize the general content of data collection instruments, it should be noted that, as designed by Hoover and Oliver , the questions are age-appropriate, some are open-ended, some are "yes or no" questions, some are "fill in the blank" questions, and some questions invite students to rate a bullying issue on a numerical scale.

EXAMPLE QUESTIONS

- A "yes or no" question: Have you been bullied during this school year?

- An open-ended question: How do you feel when you see someone being picked on?

- A "fill in the blank" question: What grade would you give your school's anti-bullying program?

- A numerical scale question: How many times in the past month have you been teased in a way you did not like?

Assessment instruments should include questions about bullying behavior, being a victim of bullying, and being a bystander to bullying. Victims are usually quick to respond to anonymous questions; they have been wanting to tell, but dared not. The same is true of bystanders; they are usually ashamed of their non-intervention and when given a non-punitive opportunity to tell, they will. It is much less likely that even on an anonymous, non-punitive questionnaire will bullies admit to their actions. Either they mistrust the anonymity guaranteed by the school staff or they truly do not believe their actions caused harm to anyone.

After all data has been collected, something meaningful must be done with it lest it sit on the principal's desk collecting dust. Hoover and Oliver suggest that the data be used to answer these questions:

- What is the prevalence of bullying in our school?

- Have we met our goals?

- How do students perceive the performance of adults in the school?

- Where is bullying occurring?

- What do students believe about bullying?

Dr. Dan Olweus advocated the use of questionnaires to collect data to determine how well a school has met these goals. He believes these questionnaires achieve the following:

- Increased awareness of the bullying/victim problem.

- Achieve active involvement on the part of teachers and parents.

- Give an absolutely clear message to the students: Bullying is not accepted in our school.

- Develop clear rules against bullying.

- Provide support and protection for victims.

To meet these goals, Olweus suggested, involves a restructuring of the school environment. Anti-bullying measures should be used at the school level, the class level, and the individual level.

Since Olweus set the initial standards for researching, preventing, and intervening in school bullying, it is fitting that he has the final word:

"How willing is our society to change this reality, so painful for so many students in a more positive direction? Considering this question, one thing should be made absolutely clear: It is no longer possible to avoid taking action about bullying problems at school using lack of knowledge as an excuse."

Remember

10.01.1997 — Pearl, Mississippi

Luke Woodham, 16, killed two students and wounded seven others.
Woodham was also accused of killing his mother. He and his friends were
said to be outcasts who worshiped Satan.

chapter nine

Bullying and the Law

"I told them what was going on. I was harassed every day, and I was afraid to go to school. I skipped school a lot and started making bad grades. I didn't get my scholarship and my parents can't afford to send me to college. I don't know what to do."
— E. K., a victim of bullying

Introduction

Creating anti-bullying school environments, eliminating the myths and stereotypes that perpetuate bullying, and establishing a zero tolerance policy on school bullying have become priorities for millions of schools across America. For some, however, these actions are too little, too late. In some schools, the worst has already happened and the bell cannot be un-rung. Parents, students, community leaders, law enforcement agencies, and legislatures are, by their actions, screaming out the window, "We're as mad as hell and we're not going to take this anymore!" When inaction or incompetent action results in serious harm or the death of a student or students, it is time to call the lawyers and the newspapers and make a lot of noise. Parents are no longer accepting platitudes and hand-wringing from school officials. Holding candlelight remembrances and well-meant grief and sympathy will not bring back Eric Harris, Dylan Klebold, and the 13 people they gunned down at Columbine High School.

In some states where parents are mad as hell, lawsuits have been filed against school officials for millions of dollars in civil actions for failure to take preventative action, deliberate indifference, and negligent supervision — and they are winning. Twenty years ago, when a police officer appeared at the door during school hours, mothers were annoyed to learn that their children went to the movies instead of going to school. Today, the sight of a police officer walking up their sidewalk freezes the hearts of every mother in America. Was it suicide or homicide? Are their children the perpetrators or the victims? *Why is my child dead?*

The Anchorage school district and its insurance company paid $4.5 million to settle a lawsuit filed by the family of a child who attempted suicide due to chronic bullying. The child has irreversible brain damage.

A pending lawsuit in Oregon seeks monetary damages and seeks to compel a school district to institute anti-bullying policies. A camera on a school bus recorded a serious incident of bullying; the child stated that he was regularly attacked in a similar manner. He even named his attackers, but the school district took no action to prevent further assaults.

In California, $1.1 million was paid in a settlement to six plaintiffs who alleged that the school failed to intervene in numerous incidents of sexual harassment because the plaintiffs were gay. One boy was beaten in full view of a school bus driver.

In Washington, a judge awarded $310,000 to a child with cerebral palsy who was bullied for more than four years by a boy who consistently called her "retard," blocked her way as she tried to pass in her wheelchair, and rammed her into walls while screaming obscenities at her.

In addition to monetary damages, district courts all over the nation are deciding cases in the plaintiffs' favor for bullying that occurred at school due to failure to provide adequate supervision, failure to intervene when a child told school counselors that they were suicidal due to bullying and did, in fact, kill themselves, failure to take preventative action in sexual harassment, deliberate indifference by a school district in allowing a racially hostile environment to exist in school, negligent supervision by allowing a "slap fight" to continue for at least ten minutes, negligent supervision by allowing students to throw rocks at another student during recess, resulting in the victim's loss of an eye, failure to protect a child who suffered a broken nose, concussion, and lacerations due to being beaten by another child, and failure to protect a child with obsessive-compulsive disorder and Tourette's Syndrome who suffered two years of bullying at school before he "snapped" and threatened violence against his tormentors.

These are only a few cases discussed by Mary Jo McGrath in her book, *School Bullying – Tools for Avoiding Harm and Liability*. As a human relations attorney, McGrath has a unique perspective on bullying and the law. Remarking on the many lawsuits filed against school districts, she theorizes that the monetary awards are occurring because many school officials, administrators, and employees are not fulfilling their duties.

This chapter examines two types of legal issues that comprise bullying:

- The three main causes of legal action, i.e. failure to take preventative action, deliberate indifference, and negligent supervision.

- Types of injuries and incidents resulting from bullying, i.e. bullying itself, suicide, threats of violence against the victim, sexual harassment, anti-gay discrimination, physical assault, verbal harassment, and civil rights violations.

If it takes a village to raise a child and it takes a nation to save one, too often it takes a jury and/or a judge to protect one.

In Loco Parentis

The law requires that school administrators and employees provide a safe educational environment for the children they supervise. When children are at school, educational personnel assume the duties and responsibilities of the children's parents, a legal concept called *in loco parentis*. School employees who fail to perform these duties cannot claim governmental immunity. In fact, in cases of deliberate indifference towards the safety of the child, school officials can be held legally liable for any physical or emotional injury suffered by a child. School employees have a legal duty to take steps, such as an anti-bullying program that works, to prevent harm to students by adequate supervision of the environment, by thoroughly investigating allegations of bullying, and by taking immediate remedial action to prevent further harm of the same type. Parents, if they were present in the school, would take these actions to prevent their children from being bullied. Under the legal doctrine of *in loco parentis*, school employees are stand-ins for parents and must use their authority to protect all children attending the school. They are legally liable, or responsible, for both preventing bullying and helping the victim(s) to recover from the effects of school bullying.

McGrath cites three bodies of law that govern bullying: (1) civil law, (2) criminal law, and (3) administrative law. A civil action is a lawsuit filed for the purpose of enforcing a civil and/or personal right. The plaintiff (the student through his or her parents) may seek monetary damages if he or she has been physically or emotionally harmed, and may also seek an injunction against any further harm by the perpetrator — the bully. In states that allow bullying-oriented lawsuits, the school employees and school district can be sued for negligent acts where harm done to the victim was foreseeable, for harassment or discrimination to which they were deliberately indifferent, and for violating the student's civil rights.

The legal duties of school officials when it comes to criminal law vary widely from state to state. Some states have enacted legislation creating a duty for school officials to protect children from assault, battery, rape, sexual abuse, hate crimes, theft, extortion, and other crimes that occur in school or during school-sponsored activities.

Bullying behavior may constitute criminal conduct. Battery, for example, is a crime comprised of unwanted and unjustified offensive touching. An assault is either an attempted or a threatened battery, a distinction not usually known by those with no legal training. Bullying behavior can be a battery, an assault, or both. For example, if another child says to your child, "Tomorrow on the bus I'm going to whip your ass," this is an assault. If the child makes good on his or her threat and physically attacks your child, this is a battery. Both are crimes. Bullying, however, is a very complex legal issue under criminal law statutes.

A Closer Look at the Juvenile Justice System and Bullying

Like the adult criminal justice system, the juvenile justice system is based upon the old English common law as administered for centuries by the king of the realm. The colonists brought the laws and legal practices with them when they came to America. It is quite simple to examine legal terminology and legal procedures today and see clearly that they still carry the ghost of English common law, especially in the case of juvenile justice. It must be emphasized that America has no nation-wide juvenile justice system, nor is there a federal court system for juveniles. Each state, then, would administer a case of bullying differently. Or some states may decline to recognize bullying as behavior that warrants the intervention of the juvenile justice system.

By law, any child under the age of majority is legally referred to as an "infant." Repeatedly, it is easy to see what wording and practices have been carried into the American juvenile justice system. A prime example is the old English common law concept of *parens patriae*. This Latin term means "father of the country." Originating in the 12th century, it applies to juveniles, in that the king has total responsibility for all matters involving juveniles. The king is a child's "father" in matters of how a child is cared for by the male head of the household and how the child is disciplined for behavioral infractions that "disturb the king's peace in the realm." In the name of the king, chancellors in various jurisdictions addressed misbehavior by a juvenile. For example, a child who continually harassed and bullied other children would appear before the local chancellor to be punished for bullying others. The chancellor, usually through public whipping or other physical manners, could discipline parents who neglected and/or abused their children. Juveniles had no legal rights of any kind or any standing in a court of law. Under *parens patriae*, children were wards of the king, yet they were the chattel, or property, of the male head of the house.

Parens patriae is still prevalent in the juvenile justice system as evidenced by a wide array of dispositions used by juvenile court judges at their discretion. Since juveniles have no Constitutional right to a jury trial; a juvenile judge can lawfully impose disciplinary actions upon juveniles that are not used in adult courts. For example, a chronic bully can be verbally reprimanded, placed on probation, ordered to attend therapy, and sent to diversion programs like DEFY (Drug Education for Youth). Failure to comply with the court's order could result in the removal of the child from the home and placed in foster care or secure placement.

In the common law, juveniles are incapable of committing crimes because, in their infancy, they are unable to form the necessary *mens rea*, or criminal intent. A *juvenile delinquent* is a child who commits an act that, if committed by an adult, would be considered a crime. Bullying, therefore, falls under the prevue of the state's juvenile justice system. There are many sanctions that a juvenile court judge can impose upon a bullying juvenile delinquent that include supervised probation, community service, boot camps, payment of restitution to the victim, house arrest, electronic monitoring, and out of home placements. A juvenile cannot be arrested, but can be *detained*. A juvenile cannot be incarcerated, but can be *placed outside the home*. For serious felonies like homicide, attempted homicide, rape, and severe battery, a juvenile can be *waivered*, or transferred into the adult criminal justice system, tried as an adult, and sentenced as an adult.

A direct opposite of the prevailing doctrine of *parens patriae* is the Get Tough Movement. While *parens patriae* sought to rehabilitate juvenile offenders, the Get Tough Movement advocates accountability and justice for juvenile offenders. Many juvenile court judges hold a juvenile delinquent entirely responsible for his or her actions; under *parens patriae* a child cannot form criminal intent and thus is not responsible for illegal acts. The Get Tough Movement would have more juveniles tried as adults and sentenced accordingly. The movement has two major flaws: (1) A child offender in an adult prison will be subjected to rape by multiple inmates; although vigilant and well-trained, correctional officers cannot possibly see everything that occurs in the prison when the inmates outnumber the correctional staff by 40 to one. A child in prison would need to be placed in administrative segregation to prevent being sexually assaulted. This increases the duties of already thinly stretched correctional officers. (2) The adult criminal courts are already seriously over-burdened. From arrest to trial could be as long as a year. If a defendant cannot post bail, or if bail is denied, he or she will be incarcerated for a lengthy time without having been found guilty of any crime. Since the Constitution guarantees the right to a speedy trial to keep this type of situation from happening, many defense attorneys file motions on behalf of the defendant, such as a writ of *habeas corpus* ("release the body") that essentially means "Take me to trial or release me."

Children who are certified as adults for a pattern of, or a single incident of, bullying behavior so extreme as to warrant a jury trial and the possibility of incarceration will wait a long time before their case comes to trial; unless they have parents financially able to post bail for them and are willing to have the child return to his or her home, these children will sit in the county jail until their trial is heard. In both jail and prison, children emerge from incarceration with no education, no social skills, no self-esteem, or sense of belonging; they have learned no empathy towards others, have learned how to victimize others, and how to commit even more crimes.

Perhaps the following **fictional** case study best illustrates how bullying would be addressed in juvenile court and in the adult criminal justice system:

CASE STUDY: FICTIONAL

Mitch is fifteen years old, in the seventh grade. He comes from a single parent home; his mother works until late at night, and Mitch is on his own most of the day. For the past two years, Mitch has been severely bullying a younger boy, Ahmed. Mitch hated Ahmed because he comes from Saudi Arabia, wears Middle Eastern clothing, practices Islam, and has a diet nothing like the other kids in school.

Ahmed, a devout Muslim, is allowed by the school to pray five times a day as required in the Koran. Mitch equates all Muslims with those who destroyed the World Trade Center. Thus, Mitch sets about a campaign to "get rid of Ahmed." Mitch bullied Ahmed in the presence of bystanders in many ways; he ripped up Ahmed's prayer rug, threw his lunch box into a ditch every day, and used a swing-blade knife to make slashes in Ahmed's white robe and red headdress. Mitch stole Ahmed's Koran from his locker and urinated all over it. He called Ahmed "rag head," "Osama," "killer," and "camel shit eater." Mitch demanded that the bystanders take part in this name-calling and taunting. Ahmed's parents were financially secure; Mitch told him, "You may have American money, but your raggedy ass is mine."

CASE STUDY: FICTIONAL

Mitch's daily bullying of Ahmed became physical, as witnessed by the bystanders who were afraid to intervene. Mitch rode the school bus with Ahmed; he threw Ahmed's books out the window, punched him in the back of the head, and tripped him as Ahmed climbed the steps to get onto the bus. The bus driver did not board the bus until it was time to depart, and observed none of this behavior. Ahmed did not tell his father, the head of the house, about the bullying because he was ashamed of letting another boy do these things to him. Mitch wrote him a note in school that said, "I'm going to do to you what your murdering people did to Americans. Tell Allah you're on your way to see him."

The next night Ahmed was walking home from the library when Mitch and four other boys abducted him and took him to the outskirts of town near the old quarry, now filled with water. Mitch stripped Ahmed naked and beat him around the head, chest, and shoulders. Then he forced Ahmed to the ground and told the four bystanders to kick and stomp him or they would "get the same thing this rag head's getting." The four boys, out of fear, complied with Mitch's instructions. When Ahmed was semi-conscious, Mitch and the other boys kept him tied up and pushed him over the ridge and into the water-filled quarry. When one of the boys said that they should check Ahmed to see if he was okay, Mitch replied, "He's nothing, nobody. I hope he's dead."

The boys went home, except for the boy that wanted to check on Ahmed. He found Ahmed barely alive, pulled him from the water, and called 911 for help. Ahmed had three broken ribs, a broken collarbone, and numerous bruises and lacerations all over his body. Ahmed's mother was an American citizen, born in the U.S.A. When Ahmed identified Mitch and the other boys, she went to the district attorney's office and requested an investigation of this matter. The DA's investigators summarized the delinquent acts committed by Mitch and the four other boys: harassment, kidnapping, assault and battery, and attempted murder in the second degree.

There are two possible ways to respond to Mitch's and the other boys' actions:

Option #1: Mitch and the bystanders were taken into the juvenile justice system. After a lengthy intake interview with all five boys, the intake officer advised the juvenile District Attorney that, in his opinion, the four bystanders were remorseful for their actions and could be rehabilitated in the juvenile justice system — the boy who rescued Ahmed and called 911 in particular. However, the intake officer advised the DA that Mitch appeared to have no remorse for his actions and should be transferred to the adult criminal justice system. The four bystanders were adjudicated as delinquent youths and ordered by the juvenile court judge to perform 100 hours of community service in a local mosque. They were also placed on strict probation that established curfew, required passing grades, giving personal apologies to Ahmed and his parents, and random drug testing. Their parents assured the judge that all orders of the court would be followed. Mitch was transferred to the adult criminal justice system; he was charged with harassment, kidnapping, assault, and battery, and first-degree attempted murder. At trial, numerous witnesses, including the four bystanders, testified about Mitch's relentless bullying of Ahmed for the preceding two years. When Ahmed testified, he stated, "My religion doesn't permit suicide unless it is for *jihad* (holy war), but I had decided to kill myself and ask Allah's forgiveness. I could no longer live with being harassed every day at school. I came to learn, not to fight. My family is against what happened on September 11th, and my father said so publicly. Why must I be hated and killed for something that was not my fault?" The jury found Mitch guilty of all charges. After a pre-sentence investigation, the judge sentenced Mitch to 15 years in a medium security prison. He would be eligible for parole in five years, at age 20.

Option #2: Mitch and the bystanders were taken into the juvenile justice system. The intake officer advised the juvenile District Attorney that all five boys could be rehabilitated as juvenile delinquents. Upon the DA's recommendation, the juvenile court judge ordered that all five boys be declared as juvenile delinquents; the four bystanders were released to their parents under strict, supervised probation. They were required to write letters of apology to Ahmed and his parents, read the Koran and study the history of Islam, write an essay on Islam, obey curfew, make passing grades in all their classes, submit to random drug tests, and meet with their probation officer twice a week. Mitch received the same sanctions, but he was also ordered to attend a six-week boot camp program to increase his self-discipline and teamwork with others. The judge told Mitch that if he failed to comply with any of these sanctions, or if he bullied other children again, he would be transferred to the adult criminal court since he cannot be rehabilitated.

This is an extreme case of bullying that involved significant physical injury to the victim and a remorseless bully who committed the crimes of an adult. The majority of bullying cases are nowhere near this severe. However, educators, parents, and those who work in juvenile and adult corrections are beginning to wonder where the line should be drawn. A victim who is constantly harassed at school is just as emotionally scarred as Ahmed would be. Somewhere, a line is crossed between bullying as relentless harassment and bullying that kills. When this occurs, parents and school personnel have the option of upping the ante into the juvenile justice system. What happens next depends on the manner in which the juvenile court judge in a particular locale interprets the facts of the case and how he or she believes the offending child can be rehabilitated.

Since there is no standardized juvenile justice system, two Midwestern cases illustrate how widely decisions about juvenile justice vary *within the same state.*

In *People vs. Sellers*, the defendant, at age fourteen, committed the first-degree murder of both his parents. He claimed that he was influenced to commit these homicides by his practice of Satanism. Sellers was tried as an adult, convicted, and executed several years later, in his twenties.

In *People vs. Snow*, the defendant, at age fourteen, became angry when a neighbor told him to stop riding his skateboard in the neighbor's driveway. Snow went into his home, obtained his father's loaded shotgun, and killed the neighbor. He was taken into the state's custody and retained in the juvenile justice system. He was placed in a maximum security out of home placement and released on his eighteenth birthday.

If cases of first-degree murder can be this nebulous and confusing, it is very difficult for lawmakers to decide where bullying behavior comes in and what to do about it. The law presumes that all offenses committed by juveniles will be handled via the juvenile justice system, unless certification is made to transfer him or her into the adult criminal justice system. Even McGrath is silent on the subject of criminalizing bullying behavior, concentrating instead on pursuing civil remedies to punish and prevent bullying. All behavior that constitutes bullying, however, has been studied by forensic specialists who strongly endorse placing bullies in front of a juvenile court judge to feel the brunt of the juvenile justice system and what could await them in the adult criminal justice system if they fail to conform their actions, as adults, to the confines of the law.

A parent who is grieving the loss of her husband, robbed at gunpoint, and then shot by a thirteen-year-old boy could decry, "What difference does it make how old my husband's killer is? Whether he's thirteen or thirty, my husband is still dead."

Administration

The third body of law that regulates the actions of school employees is administrative law. According to McGrath, administrative law includes, but is not limited to, policies, procedures, and regulations of:

- The school district's governing board.

- Federal regulatory agencies, such as the Office for Civil Rights.

- The state's education code, government code, and administrative regulations.

School employees *must* know and implement the school district's policies and procedures on bullying if they exist. As agents of the government, school employees are charged with the responsibility of enforcing anti-bullying codes. Failure to do so could result in civil actions for damages (actual and punitive) due to negligent supervision, deliberate indifference, or failure to protect students against bullying.

Negligence Defined

When used in a legal context, negligence is defined as the failure to act as a reasonable person is expected to act in similar circumstances, when a duty exists toward the person affected. In simple terms, negligence involves a school employee's failure to act to prevent bullying and protect victims when they have a duty toward students to do this. The "reasonable person" test is common in the law: Would any reasonable person, in a similar circumstance, intervene to prevent bullying and protect victims? The legal doctrine of *in loco parentis* generates a school employee's legal duty towards students since they accept responsibility for the students during school hours and school-sponsored activities.

McGrath gives a four-point test to illustrate how courts determine whether an educator or administrator is negligent in bullying cases:

- Did the educator have a legal duty to the injured student?

- Did the educator fail to fulfill this duty?

- Was there an injury to the person to whom the educator had a duty?

- Did the educator's failure to fulfill the duty directly or proximately cause the injury?

For students, through their parents, to bring a civil cause of action against school employees based on negligence, the answers to all four of these questions must be "yes." In bullying cases, juries have found in favor of the plaintiff primarily due to negligence by school employees.

CASE STUDY: MARY J.

Mary J. has a cleft palate that was surgically repaired when she was very young, but the procedure left a permanent scar on her upper lip, and she attends speech therapy at school because of her difficulty pronouncing certain words and sounds.

At age 16, Mary was a student at the local high school. She was a good student with no record of disciplinary problems and was generally liked by her classmates. However, this year a new girl, Greta, enrolled in the school and was in several classes with Mary. Greta launched a bullying campaign against Mary because of her disability. Every day, Greta called Mary names in front of other students, e.g. "scarface," "rabbit lip," "mumbles," "butt ugly," and "speech freak." This occurred in the hallways and the cafeteria, as well as at school-sponsored activities, like soccer games and science fairs.

When Mary tried out for, and won, a part in a school play, Greta repeatedly said, in front of other students and the drama teacher, "You guys must really be desperate if you let 'gross lips' into the play." She offered students a dollar if they would boycott the play with her; some students, out of fear, complied with Greta's demand. Two of these students reported Greta's bullying to the school counselor, who did not talk with Mary or Greta, and did not inform the principal about Mary being bullied. One day Mary was standing at her school locker and Greta slammed the metal locker door into her face, causing Mary to have cuts on her face and mouth. She went to the school nurse to have her injuries tended, and told the nurse how she was hurt and details of Greta's constant bullying. She also told the nurse that she cried every day before school and thought about committing suicide.

The nurse did not report the bullying to the principal or any other school official, nor did she inform Mary's parents that Mary was being bullied and had suicidal ideation. A week later, Greta again slammed the locker door into Mary's face; this time Mary lost one of her front teeth. Mary's parents insisted on knowing exactly how Mary was injured, why the school's anti-bullying

CASE STUDY: MARY J.

policy was not followed, and why three school employees failed to report that Mary was being bullied by Greta. Mary required dental surgery to insert a false front tooth and received 29 stitches in her mouth, which she found to be very painful. After discussing the situation with her parents, Mary filed a lawsuit, through her parents, against the school for negligent supervision.

In pre-trial depositions, it was discovered that the school hallways were not supervised after classes by adults and that another student had previously reported being physically bullied in the hallway. The school's zero tolerance for bullying policy was up-to-date and well constructed. At least in Mary's case, it was not followed. At trial, the jury found that school employees had a legal duty to Mary under the concept of *in loco parentis*, that school employees failed to fulfill this duty, that Mary was injured emotionally and physically on school property, and that Mary's physical and emotional injury was the result of school employees' failure to protect her. The jury also found that the drama teacher, the school counselor, and the school nurse were personally liable for Mary's injuries because they received notice that Mary was being bullied, that these individuals demonstrated a pattern of deliberate indifference for the bullying, that they failed to take remedial action, and that their failure to do these things caused injury to Mary.

The jury awarded Mary $10,000 actual damages for her dental surgery and her twice-weekly sessions with a therapist. They awarded her an additional one million dollars in punitive damages for the deliberate indifference of the drama teacher, the school counselor, and the school nurse and also for negligent supervision of the hallways between classes. The judge ordered that Greta be remanded to the juvenile justice system for adjudication as a juvenile delinquent and to be rehabilitated.

Although this is a **fictional** example, it contains all the necessary elements of civil liability that are attached when a school fails in its duty to provide a safe, bully-free environment for students.

What is probably most disturbing about this example is that the school had a workable anti-bullying program that could easily have been effective in protecting Mary and preventing her physical and emotional harm by Greta. It is distressing when, after the spotlight has focused intently on bullying because of the subsequent bullycides and school shooting, a school fails to adopt a zero tolerance for bullying program. It is reprehensible when a school has such a policy and negligently fails to implement it, causing serious harm or even death for a student.

> *When you have the law on your side, you pound the law.*
> *When you have the facts on your side, you pound the facts.*
> *When you have neither the law nor the facts on your side,*
> *you pound the table.*
> *— A Lawyer's Proverb*

In cases of civil liability in bullying episodes, there is a lot of table pounding by the school's lawyers to relieve the school of its duties to prevent and remediate harm to students caused by bullying. For example, anti-bullying policies that prohibit name-calling, verbal degradation, or verbal abuse are not violations of the bully's First Amendment right of free speech. Nor does prohibiting mob bullying violate the group's right to assemble. Perhaps one day we will see a defense to a school shooting based upon the Constitutional right to bear arms.

To date, 23 states have enacted anti-bullying legislation, and 15 more state legislatures have introduced similar bills. Washington state's legislation is often used as an example of a well-constructed anti-bullying law. McGrath notes that this particular statute received an "A" rating from **www.bullypolice.org**, a Web site devoted to tracking and evaluating the effectiveness of state anti-bullying legislation.

At the time McGrath was crafting her book on the legal aspects of bullying, she notes that there was a bill in Congress known as the Anti-Bullying Act of 2005. This act would require districts and schools to prevent and respond to instances of bullying and harassment as part of an on-going effort to ensure the safety of students at school. This bill, HR 284, was sponsored by 40 legislators and was referred to the Subcommittee on Education Reform. The bill requires schools to have discipline policies against bullying and harassment, to establish complaint procedures for students and parents, and to notify parents on a yearly basis of new anti-bullying policies and procedures adopted by the school. To date, HR 284 has not been passed, still being buried in the subcommittee no-man's land. **Write your congressional representative!**

Stalking as a Form of Bullying

A general legal definition of stalking is comprised of three elements: (1) a pattern of behavioral intrusion upon another person that is unwanted, (2) an implicit or explicit threat that is evidenced in the pattern of behavioral intrusion, and (3) as a result of these intrusions, the person who is threatened experiences reasonable fear. In other words, stalking is the willful, malicious, and repeated following and harassing of another person that threatens his or her safety.

Adults stalking other adults is not only thoroughly researched and discussed in psychological and legal literature. The "Madonna stalker" and the "David Letterman stalker" made headlines the world over. Stalking that is associated with domestic violence is very well documented, as is stalking by persons who suffer from serious personality disorders and delusional disorders.

Even some serial killers have been dubbed as stalkers, such as Richard Ramirez, nicknamed "The Night Stalker." Adult stalkers and their victims fill the talk shows and forensic documentaries, as well as fictional TV dramas like "CSI:" and all the incarnations of "Law and Order."

An examination of stalking associated with bullying by school-age children yields no results. Stalking is considered to be an adult issue, yet there seems to be no reason, legal or otherwise, to exclude stalking from the accepted definitions of bullying. Other crimes, such as homicide, rape, and battery are a prominent part of the child bully's lexicon; why stalking has been excluded is a mystery. The general description of stalking, as noted above, encompasses acts that can easily be perpetrated by school age bullies. If children are capable of committing murder, they are certainly capable of committing stalking. The best way of demonstrating stalking as bullying is through a **fictional case study**:

CASE STUDY: NATALIE

Natalie is a fourteen-year-old student at her local middle school. She is an attractive, popular girl who consistently makes good grades and participates in many school-sponsored activities. Natalie rides the school bus to and from school each day and eats lunch in the school cafeteria. Although her parents do not allow her to date yet, she is friendly with a few same-age boys in her classes, and has been allowed to have them over for dinner and a movie at her parents' home as long as they are present.

Natalie obeys her parents' curfew and is not a discipline problem at home or school. One day Natalie noticed a boy on the school bus who had not previously ridden the bus. She was seated near the back of the bus; the boy was several rows in front of her but had turned around in his seat and was staring at Natalie, which unnerved her a bit. Natalie

CASE STUDY: NATALIE

did not have any classes with this boy, but she started seeing him frequently in the school hallways and in the cafeteria at lunchtime. He always seemed to be staring at her. The boy appeared to be about her age, was always neatly dressed, and was pleasant-looking. Natalie never saw the boy in the presence of other students, either boys or girls, and he didn't appear to talk to anyone.

On the bus one morning, the boy sat down next to Natalie and introduced himself as Shane. Natalie felt mildly uncomfortable with Shane sitting next to her; he never took his eyes off her. Shane stated, "You are going to be my girlfriend" in an emphatic tone of voice. Natalie didn't respond and looked straight ahead. From that day on, Natalie saw Shane everywhere she went; on the bus to and from school, at soccer games, in the hallways, in the cafeteria, and in the gym.

She never spoke to him, nor he to her. He was simply there. Her male friends stopped talking with her; she asked one of them if anything was wrong and he replied, "You know that guy Shane? He told me he'd stick a knife in my throat if I didn't leave you alone. He said the same thing to Mike and Stan." Natalie realized that Shane was isolating her from her friends, controlling who she could talk with and be with. She didn't tell her parents about Shane because she thought she might be over-reacting.

One day she found a note taped to her locker that said, "I'm always watching out for you." It was unsigned, but Natalie knew it was from Shane. Over the next week, she often found similar notes and a flower taped to her locker. One of the notes had only her address and phone number on it, as if Shane wanted her to know that he knew exactly where she lived. She began to receive "anonymous" e-mails and text messages on her cell phone. By this time Natalie was very frightened of Shane; he had started to follow her in the halls and sit near her on the bus. She saw him at every school activity she attended.

One afternoon on the school bus, Shane sat down beside her and said, "Here are the rules. I'm your boyfriend, and you won't

CASE STUDY: NATALIE

talk to any other guys. I don't want you playing soccer anymore; your shorts are too tight, and boys are looking at you. I don't want you hanging around with Debbie anymore, either. I heard she's a slut. I'll call your cell phone every night at eight, and you better answer. I'll know if you're not home, too. You better not tell your parents; I don't want to have to hurt them. Understand? I love you, and that's it."

Natalie was terrified. Strange things began to happen; she talked to Debbie in a chat room, and the next day her dog was shot with a BB gun in the leg. She participated in the soccer play-off game, and the next day found her soccer uniform ripped and slashed with a sharp instrument. Her science book disappeared from her securely locked locker, and then reappeared three days later. Shane had discovered her lock's combination.

Finally, Natalie could take no more; she told her parents everything that had occurred. They contacted the school principal the next morning, and the principal contacted the police and Shane's mother, a single parent. In a conference, Shane's mother told him not to speak, and she denied that her son had stalked Natalie. Shane was detained by the police for violation of the state's stalking laws and was taken to the juvenile justice detention center for booking. He was released into his mother's custody. At her parents' insistence, Natalie attended a private, all-girl school for the rest of that school year. Shane was adjudicated as a juvenile delinquent and placed on strict probation that prohibited him from having contact with Natalie in any form, and from harassing her in any way. He was expelled from school for violating the school's anti-bullying policy. Natalie never heard from or saw Shane again.

This fictional example contains all three legal elements of stalking. It also violates every anti-bullying program included in this book. Invading another's personal space is bullying. Destroying the property of others is bullying. Threatening another person is bullying. Intimidating and controlling another person is bullying. All these actions have something in common: They are all forms of both bullying and stalking. By this reasoning, *stalking another student should be incorporated into definitions of bullying*. Since stalking can be either same-sex or cross-gender, it is applicable to all forms of bullying, including cyberbullying that most often occurs among girls.

Although stalking is usually committed in order to terrorize and intimidate the victim, there are many examples of stalking that turns deadly (Meloy, 1998). This, too, can be applied to children because they are no strangers to homicide, as evidenced by school shootings and individual first-degree murders. The outdated notion that children are unable to form criminal intent has been challenged many times by the facts of cases of aggravated violence upon children by children. To leave stalking out of the definition of bullying is to ignore behavior that is both terrorizing and pre-meditated. To include stalking as a bullying behavior requires a change in our thinking about what constitutes bullying. Failure to accept this as necessary puts at risk the physical and emotional safety of all school–age children.

"Change is the law of life. Those who look only to the past or the present are certain to miss the future."
– President John F. Kennedy

Hate Crimes and Bullying

Violence perpetrated by one person upon another person is a crime. Hate crimes are especially insidious because they are an attack upon who we are as Americans and individuals. Our Constitution tells us that all men are created equal. To paraphrase author George Orwell, "…but some are more equal than others." Women and children were once the "chattel," or property, of the male head of the household. He could do with them as he wished, just as he would his farm animals. Women could not vote, own land, or enter into a legal contract. Children could be viciously beaten upon any whim of the master of the house. Long before the obscene buying and selling of human beings occurred with regularity in the colonies, women and children were being treated worse than animals.

The truth is, unless the reader is a Native American, we are all invaders of North America, having no moral right to cast aspersions upon another person's heritage. Spics, micks, niggers, chinkies, dagos, wops, sheenies, slopes, ragheads, gooks, krauts, limeys, frogs; we never seem to run out of nasty things to call each other even though, as Mahatma Gandi said of British rule in India, "You are masters of someone else's house. It is time you went home." What worked in India for the Hindus and the Muslims is not going to work for the Native Americans. It is too late.

"Can't we all just get along?"
– Rodney King

Long after the Supreme Court ended segregation in *Brown vs. the Board of Education* in 1964, and the Governor of Alabama, George Wallace, barred the schoolhouse door to keep black students from entering, the hate crimes continue. Only now, in addition to racial violence, hate crimes also include gay and lesbian targets and non-Christians. It must be emphasized that these are not "adults only" crimes. Hate activities extend to our youth as well. Members of hate groups raise their children to take pride in their hatred of other races and religions. In fact, hate crimes play a definitive role in school bullying yet is all but absent from the literature. Since children are legally incapable of committing crimes, their actions are delinquent in nature.

CASE STUDY: SUSAN AND BEAU C.

Susan and Beau are fifteen-year-old fraternal twins attending the same high school, ninth grade, in a Southern state. They are white, from a modest home, with both mother and father raising them. Their father works as a miner, and their mother is a homemaker. They have no other siblings.

Mr. C. is an avid member of the Aryan Brotherhood, a white supremacist radical organization that advocates racial segregation, and believes that whites are superior to African Americans or any other "mongrel" group. Mrs. C. is also an AB member. Both parents have raised their children as white supremacists, teaching them to hate all races except their own, and also to hate homosexuals. Susan and Brian were suspended from school on the same day after they were discovered cutting superficial gashes on the back of a younger African American student while other white students watched and cheered. They came to the mental health clinic for evaluation as part of the requirements for them to return to school. They were accompanied by their mother and father in the interview.

Susan: I'm not sorry, and I'm not going to say I'm sorry. That nigger needed a lesson in how his slave ancestors were treated, so we taught his ass that lesson. I told him that two hundred years ago, my relatives owned his relatives and beat the shit out of them whenever they wanted. That's what needs to happen in America now. Get rid of the niggers. They're all pimps and druggies. I'd rather die a slow death than have sex with a nigger.

Beau: Look, we're AB (Aryan Brotherhood). This is our life and others can just butt out, especially niggers and Jews. This is a white country that's being taken over by mongrel trash. We celebrate Hitler's birthday because he had the right idea. Get rid of the Catholics, Jews, and anyone else who wasn't all white, like the niggers and the spics. I'm peaceful as long as those MS13's (an Hispanic gang) leave me alone. Unless they want to wake up with their throats cut.

Therapist: Do you want to go back to school? I'm asking both of you.

CASE STUDY: SUSAN AND BEAU C.

Mr. C: Hold it. They aren't deciding that. I am. And I say they're going to be home schooled by my wife who will give them proper guidance about their race. No more Jap schoolteachers, no more (expletive) spic principal. My son was recently made a real Skinhead (a male youth hate group), and in a few years I'll personally swear him into the Brotherhood. Susan's got an AB boyfriend in jail for kicking the crap out of some fag. He's leader of the AB in there. When he gets out next year, they'll be married as soon as I can do it.

Therapist: If you're sure you don't want your children to return to school, then why are you here? You didn't have to keep this appointment under those circumstances.

Mr. C: Because we want people to know the truth about what happened.

Therapist: And that is?

Mrs. C: That nigger was looking at Susan in a way she didn't like. She told me, and I told her Daddy. For the best part of a year now, they been doing things to get that nigger to give her up but he wouldn't. So he got what he needed.

Therapist: Susan, what kind of things did you do?

Susan: Me and Beau and our friends, we knocked his books around, called him an ape, told him to go back and swing in the trees with his grandparents, called him "nigger lips" and lots of other names. We bought him a watermelon and told him he could go pick cotton instead of going to school since apes can't learn. Once we had him crying, and wasn't that a good one! You know that black holiday like Christmas the niggers made up?

Therapist: Do you mean Kwanza?

Susan: Yeah, that's it. That ain't a real religion, it's just something the niggers made up instead of having a white person's Christmas. And those stupid names, like Kenisha, Tawani, Mabumbo and shit? Those ain't real names. They just want to sound African. Well, if they all like Africa so much, they can take their asses over there.

CASE STUDY: SUSAN AND BEAU C.

Mr. C: Look, we know the mongrels ain't going anywhere. But white people have got to have pride enough to stand up for their country. We're proud to be white, and we're proud to be in the AB. When the race war happens, the mongrels don't stand a chance.

Beau: Dad, what about Rita?

Mr. C: What about Rita? She's half-spic. There's your answer.

Therapist: Beau, who is Rita?

Mr. C: We don't need to talk about her. She's not pure white, so she's out.

Therapist: Beau?

Mrs. C: Passing and being ain't the same.

Beau: I'm not dealing with niggers or Jews. But Rita's almost white; she don't look spic at all.

Mrs. C: Doesn't matter. You want spic-looking babies?

Beau: No ma'am, I guess not. She's just nice, and could pass for white.

Therapist: I'd like for Beau and Susan to talk more about what happened with the black student.

Susan: Well, we're not the only ABs in the school. Lots of us around here. We all gave this nigger pure hell. We stole everything he had, like his lunch money and his books and stuff. We set his football uniform on fire one night in the middle of the football field. Well, Beau and his friends did that. See, I told everybody that he was trying to be nice with me, and they took over. Wasn't no place in school that nigger could go without being spit on, tripped, called names, and once Billy J. told him he was going to (expletive) his sister like the whore she was. He had plenty of warning. All he had to do was lay low, but he didn't. He kept on smiling at me and wearing those nigger baggy clothes. Listening to that "gangsta" jungle music about drugs, guns, and stuff. My mom says that any nigger down here with a gun is gonna be one dead nigger.

CASE STUDY: SUSAN AND BEAU C.

Mrs. C. You trying to tell us that all that filthy rap stuff is real music? It's all about killing, sex, beating up women, and killing cops. They get real rich from it, too.

Mr. C: We don't hold with that down here in the deep South. Niggers had better keep to their place if they want to live here. We don't want their drugs and their gangs and white people being afraid of them. We're not afraid, and I'll raise my kids not to be afraid, either. Niggers that don't know their place are going to get just what this one got, or worse. Same for fags and Jews. We don't want their kind here. Fags are against God, unnatural.

Beau: (laughing) We had this fag in school once, name of Van, but we all called him Darling. He wore girls' clothes after school. Couldn't wear them during school because it wasn't allowed. One time we found him in gym class wearing a bra under his clothes. Oh man, was that funny! We hung his bra from the gym flagpole with a sign that said "Darling's bra" on it. We beat the crap out of him one night after the football game. I can't say what else went on because my Dad said not to. But he said he was proud of us. His parents said they were gonna sue the school board. But he did wear eye make-up and crap like that. Earrings. He was the only fag in school. In the whole town. They left town a while later.

Mr. C.: My kids are staying true to their raising. If his mother and I have to choose between what's right and what that school wants, we'll take what's right.

This harrowing case study is truly frightening in many ways. Although it is **fiction**, it could very easily be real. Not only does it set this microcosm of society back several hundred years, but is also calls attention to the fact that racial bullying is alive and thriving in public schools, and it is being taught to children by their parents. African Americans, Jews, Catholics, homosexuals, Hispanics, and other ethnic groups with pride in their own heritage are under siege by hate crime bullying in school by white youths. In other schools, the tables are turned, and white students are at a distinct disadvantage in non-segregated schools. Much of the literature on bullying refers to white students rather than minorities. The United States Supreme Court has not, as yet, established the right of states to criminalize hate-based crimes as a separate criminal law issue; our society already has laws against homicide, harassment, assault, and battery. The issue at stake is whether we need special hate crime legislation that protects minorities. Whether one agrees with this position or not, hate-based bullying is running rampant in public schools that are funded by the American taxpayer. Like stalking, it is a form of bullying that warrants further research.

Bullying and Gangs

This is another topic that requires further research. Youth gangs, by their very nature, commit acts of mob bullying upon those school-age children who are not members of the gang. The literature on youth gangs and youths involved in adult gangs are well documented by Champion (2007), Flowers (2002), Davis (2003), and Bernstein (1996). Most state Departments of Corrections issue a confidential report to penitentiary staff on the gangs active within the state and within the prison. Youth gangs and juvenile members of adult gangs are responsible for an enormous amount of crimes in drug trafficking, weapons trafficking, assault and battery, attempted homicide, manslaughter, and homicide. However, the school-age gang member's bullying actions have not yet been addressed in the literature. The concept of hate crimes and gang bullying are intertwined; the juvenile gang member does hate his or her victim, but their bullying takes a different form from strictly hate crime bullying.

Champion described three types of juvenile gangs: the scavenger gang, the territorial gang, and the corporate gang. Scavenger gangs form primarily from a need for socialization and mutual protection. Territorial gangs serve to protect their "turf" from intrusion by other gangs and non-gang youths. Corporate gangs are the most violent of the three; they are actively involved in criminal activities that mimic the behavior of adult gangs that they hope to be affiliated with when they are older. Champion cites the 1995 National Youth Gang Survey that identified nine types of gangs present in America today:

- Juvenile gangs

- Street gangs

- Taggers (loosely organized gangs)

- Drug using and selling gangs

- Satanic gangs

- Posses (local gangs)

- Crews

- Stoners

- Terrorist groups

Any of these gang sub-types has the potential to be involved in school bullying. Among juvenile gang members, harassing "enemy" gang members and children not involved in a gang is not only expected, it is *required* if a child wants to make a name for himself among the adult gangs. Children at school proudly wear the gang's colors, show the gang's tattoos, and are proficient in the passwords and hand signals of their gang. Their manner of behavior is tough, intimidating, intolerant of others, and "bad." They must never show weakness, unwillingness to fight and carry weapons, or appear vulnerable in any way. Given the extreme violence of adult gangs, it is likely that schools are a proving ground for juveniles who aspire to membership in an adult gang. Bullying other children provides gang members with "practice" violence that will greatly escalate in adult gangs. Bullying desensitizes juvenile gang members to the suffering of their victims, and the gang members who are bystanders learn to support another member's violent actions. Bullying at school becomes, then, a school of crime and violence.

Rival gang bullying is a "given" when more than one juvenile gang exists in a school. Sometimes gangs form profitable alliances, and at other times, rival gangs resort to all-out warfare on and off school grounds and during school-sponsored activities. Mob bullying best describes what occurs in these situations; one "shot caller," who leads a gang, directs his crew to harass and physically assault rival gang members. In juvenile gang warfare, the weapon of choice is "skin" or physical fist fighting. More often, a gang member finds himself in the unfortunate position of being alone, without his crew to back him up, with members of a rival gang. This is the most dreaded situation that could befall a gang member, yet he is expected to put up a good fight even though he is grossly outnumbered. The inevitable "beat down" consists of one or more members of the rival gang perpetrating a serious physical assault upon the lone "gangsta." The outcome is preordained. However, the victim of this type of mass bullying gains status in his own gang for putting up the best fight he could under the circumstances. His cuts, bruises, and even broken bones are badges of honor within the gang. Gang members are not going to report this kind of bullying to school officials; it is expected that they will cope with it on their own. Nor is the mob bullying reported to the victim's parents since they too are most likely affiliated with a gang; a parent of a "beat down" would thus be proud of his or her son for defending himself with honor.

There are, according to the Montana Department of Corrections, six reasons why school-age children join gangs:

- Lack of acceptance within their family.

- Lack of a positive adult role model in their lives.

- Protection from rival gangs.

- Achieving status and recognition among other gang members.

- The opportunity for financial gain through illegal activities.

- The glorification of gangs by the American media in movies and music.

Of these six motivations, bullying is most associated with achieving status and recognition among their own gang members and rival gangs as well. Through bullying, school-age gang members hone their skills in cruelty, lack of empathy for others, brutality, and strictly obeying the law of silence, *omerta*. They also learn that failure to support and lie for fellow gang members if one is caught doing bullying behavior is severely punished; in adult gangs, this would result in the execution of the offending member. Mastering these skills through bullying teaches juvenile "gangstas" what will be expected from him in an adult gang. A solid reputation as a bully and a supportive bystander can earn the juvenile a coveted membership in an adult gang, such as the following:

- Folk Nation

- Vice Lords

- Latin Kings

- Crips

- Bloods

- Surenos

- MS13

- Mexican Mafia

- Nortenos

- Asian Tongs

- Aryan Brotherhood

It should be noted that the Crips, an African American gang with many juvenile members, are specifically involved in extortion, assaults, and robberies *in high schools* in South Central Los Angeles. The Aryan Brotherhood is a white supremacist group that operates both on the streets and in prisons all across the county; they are considered to be the most dangerous gang in America today. Juvenile members are usually Skinheads who chant about "white power" and celebrate the birthday of Adolph Hitler. Skinheads are prevalent in schools in the south and in large urban areas. Their violent actions against Jews, African Americans, Hispanics, Muslims, Asians, and any non-white schoolchildren are legend. This is bullying at its height and most dangerous form. Juveniles aspire to wear the coveted spider web tattoo on their left elbow, signifying that the Skinhead has severely injured a non-white. A spider web that is shaded in light grey means that the wearer has killed a non-white. Gays, lesbians, and Catholics receive similar treatment from the Aryan Brotherhood and the juvenile Skinheads. A non-white, non-Christian, non-heterosexual schoolchild's worst nightmare is to encounter a gang of Skinheads on or off school grounds, including the school bus. "Bullying" is a word hardly accurate in defining what happens to these children.

- A 12-year-old Jewish child was discovered on the school athletic field with his penis cut off, nearly bleeding to death. A sign placed around his neck said, "Kike circumcision."

- A 9-year-old African American girl had the initials "AB" carved into her forehead. She named four Skinheads who locked her in a school cleaning closet and assaulted her.

- A 17 year-old gay white boy was repeatedly bullied by a Skinhead gang in school; in public, he was called "fag," "butt bomber," "race traitor," and "dick diver." He was harassed on the school bus by gang members who tore up his textbooks and notebooks, refused to allow him to sit down, and stomped on his feet with their combat boots. He was removed from school following a severe beating at a school function.

There is no justification for not including juvenile gang activity in schools in the lexicon of bullying behavior. Because it is extreme in violence and hate, it still fits the definition of bullying by Dr. Dan Olweus. Gang members show all the "red flag" indicators of bullying children. Their victims are vulnerable, different in some way, and unable to fight back against a wave of such venomous, indoctrinated bullies. The behavior of African American, Asian, and Hispanic juvenile gang members at school is no different from that of the Aryan Brotherhood and the Skinheads they spawned. Even female juvenile and adult gang members, or "SOS" (Sisters of the Struggle), can be relentless, remorseless bullies on behalf of their gang, bringing the concept of "mean girls" to a new height of cruelty within the school.

It is therefore essential for school personnel to know what juvenile gangs are present in their school, in what number, and what illegal activities they are involved in, such as drug trafficking. *Every incident of bullying should be forensically examined by a gang expert, preferably a staff member, to determine if the bullying bears signs of being gang-related.* Every police department in a fair-sized town has a gang expert. If one is not present in the town, the state police's office will gladly send their gang expert to assist in the investigation of the incident.

A checklist for school personnel in considering whether a bullying incident is gang-related should include:

- The ethnicity of the victim.

- The religion of the victim.

- The type of injuries suffered by the victim.

- The presence of gang-related graffiti near the site of the incident.

- The presence of written "calling cards," like signs left on or near the victim.

- A statement by the victim, unless he or she is too intimidated to make a statement.

- Previous reports of similar incidents.

- Reports of gang activity in the school by students and forensic local gang experts.

Finally, to close our eyes to gang violence as a form of bullying is to condemn our school-age children to the relentless attacks of merciless juvenile gang members who wish to divide the nation by color, ethnic background, or religion. The U.S. Constitution directly contradicts this perversion of the rights of every individual, juvenile schoolchild, or adult.

"Wherever I go, whatever I do, someone is going to disapprove of me. So I have decided to just be myself and let others worry about whether or not I belong."
– C.J. Oldman

Bullying as Legally Actionable Behavior

America is known as a litigious society; we will sue just about anybody for just about anything. Our courts are hopelessly clogged with frivolous lawsuits that, unfortunately, must be addressed. The courts are available to every citizen who wishes to resolve a dispute regardless of the lack of merit or downright silliness of the plaintiff's complaint against the defendant. Although some district courts are refusing to hear frivolous cases filed in large numbers by a particular citizen, this is a dangerous practice. Legal by state laws, it is one person – a judge – who decides what cases should be heard. In our long history, only the U.S. Supreme Court can determine what cases it will or will not hear.

Research indicates that some types of bullying are legally actionable under both civil and criminal law. Lest these cases be considered frivolous, McGrath outlines a five-point checklist to determine whether a single bullying incident or continuous harassment meets the criteria for legal merit:

ONE TIME INCIDENT VERSUS CONTINUOUS HARASSMENT	
1	**Is a protected classification involved or is there an intent to harm?** If bullying is directed towards a member of a protected class of people, such as children in school or participating in school-sponsored activities, the bully's behavior can be addressed as illegal harassment and discrimination. The crucial question in bullying is, *Did the perpetrator intend to cause harm to the victim?*
2	**Is the behavior unwelcome or unwanted?** Two children engaging in a mutual "slap fight" may be silly, but it is not bullying. One child striking another in an unwanted manner constitutes bullying.
3	**Is the behavior severe, persistent, or pervasive?** To constitute legally actionable bullying, behavior must fall into one of these categories.
4	**Does the behavior meet both subjective and objective tests related to its level of interference with student education?** Subjectively, the victim's experiences must be unreasonable interference. Objectively, any reasonable person in the same situation would feel that his or her education suffered because of this interference.
5	**Does the behavior substantially interfere with the victim's education?** It must be proven that the bully's behavior unreasonably interferes with the victim's ability to get an education. For example, if a bullying victim is afraid to attend school or cannot concentrate on schoolwork because of being bullied, this is legally actionable since all American children have the right to attend public schools.

To review, McGrath wrote that the five-point criteria determine whether some bullying behavior is legally actionable harassment and/or discrimination. It can also be used to determine whether the school is negligent or indifferent to harm caused to the victim by the bully. While it is not possible for a school to prevent lawsuits, it is certainly possible to have a lawsuit dismissed or for a jury to find in the school's favor if the lawsuit is without merit or the plaintiff student cannot meet the required burden of proof.

Finally, McGrath stresses the importance of putting an anti-bullying policy in writing in very clear and reasonable terms. The proverb "if you didn't write it down, it didn't happen" is particularly applicable in establishing a school's zero tolerance for bullying.

Conclusion

Most of the actions that constitute bullying are illegal and/or actionable in civil law, including stalking. In investigating an incident or pattern of bullying, McGrath advocates the FICA standard:

- What are the **Facts**? What happened?

- What was the **Impact** of the perpetrator(s) behavior upon the victim?

- What was the **Context**? What were the circumstances of the alleged bullying?

- What **Action** was taken by the school in response to the alleged bullying?

Schools have an absolute duty to provide a safe environment for all students; have a policy, put it in writing, and follow it. By taking these simple and reasonable steps, schools not only protect the victims of bullying, but also protect the school from emotional, occupational, and financial liability.

Remember

03.24.1998 — Jonesboro, Arkansas

Mitchell Johnson, 13, and Andrew Golden, 11, killed four students and one teacher and wounded ten others outside Westside Middle School. The boys pulled the fire alarm to empty the school and then shot classmates from the woods.

Conclusion

"Let us not look backward in anger, or forward in fear, but around in awareness."
— James Thurber

This book concludes in the same manner that it began: with the roll call of the dead.

Manchester, England. January 1999: Eight-year-old Marie Bentham hanged herself in her bedroom with her jump rope because she could no longer face being bullied at school. She is Britain's youngest bullycide.

Invercargill, New Zealand. August 1997. Fifteen-year-old Matt Ruddenklau committed suicide. The coroner's report stated, "Bullying and victimization were a significant factor in the boy's life in the months leading up to his suicide."

Victoria, British Columbia. November 1997. Fourteen-year-old Reena Virk died after being lured by schoolmates, attacked, and beaten unconscious. Reena's arm, neck, and back were deliberately broken before she was dumped into the Gorge Inlet. Reena had tried to belong to the peer group, desperately wanting to fit in. She was regularly mocked and taunted about her brown skin and her weight. *Hundreds of students knew about the relentless bullying **and her death** before someone tipped off the police.*

These are our children. They are not Jeffrey Dahmer, Ted Bundy, Richard Ramirez, or Charles Manson. We send them to school, where it was once safe in our own school days. Today, it seems that schools have become combat arenas replete with psy-ops and physical beat-downs. The combatants make use of the most up-to-date technological advances to torment their targets while others stand and watch, terrified to intervene lest they be the next target. *Omerta*, the rule of silence, is the only rule that matters.

The *Encarta* dictionary defines terrorism as "violence or the threat of violence carried out for political purposes." The original concept of terrorism was that of acts of violence, kidnapping, bombing, and other forms of fear-inducing acts by warring nations. Schools are extremely political in their own way; they determine the social politics of these microcosms. Bullying, in all its forms, has become social terrorism.

The Columbine school shootings should awaken the conscience of America just as September 11, 2001 opened our eyes to the fact that our enemies will go to any lengths to make us afraid. To wage war with the radical Middle Eastern terrorists, our nation has an arsenal of weapons and well-trained soldiers to crush the enemy and bring to justice those who murdered our people. Thousands of innocent Americans died on 9/11/01. Reena Virk died in November, 1997. Just one child. Unless we understand that bullying in our schools is social terrorism and regard the loss of children dead by bullycide or homicide as seriously as we regard those who died in the World Trade Center, the Pentagon, and in a field in Pennsylvania — heroes, all — the children will remain at risk. Heroes also are the teachers, the principals, the school district administrators, and the parents who have taken a stand on zero tolerance for bullying. The passengers of Flight 93, knowing their fate, saved hundreds, perhaps thousands of lives by sacrificing their own on September 11, 2001. In the equally serious war on bullying in our schools, many courageous students find the nerve to stand up and shout, "I'm as mad as hell, and I'm not going to take this anymore!" We have a choice: We can follow their lead or we can stand and watch as more children either die or suffer irreparable emotional harm.

The stories and vignettes contained in this book are based upon actual incidents and people. They are people just like us and just like our children. Bully, victim, or bystander — they are our children. The problem seems so complex, it may be difficult to know even where to start, but here follow some suggestions:

Know and monitor what our children are doing on the computer. Check often. Homework is good. Cyberbullying is not.

Watch children for signs of bullying, being a victim of bullying, or being a bystander of bullying. After reading this book, parents and teachers know what to look for. If we do not act upon what we see and what our gut instincts tell us, we have failed as parents. Our children pay the price of our failure.

Schools *must* have a workable, clearly understood, at least annually reviewed policy for anti-bullying. If this does not happen, a school must be subject to legal action for any ruthless bullying that causes harm to a child. Sometimes people only listen and act when the judge bangs his gavel, establishing moral and civil guilt. If that is what it takes, do it.

Teachers, parents, other adults — *talk to the children*. They may have been afraid to tell us, but may eagerly take the opportunity to do so if they feel safe, supported, and believed. Perhaps even the bullies want to stop, but do not know how. Punishment here is not the answer; the "reformed" bullies must be accountable for their actions, and apologies are definitely in order; allow them to change. Allow others to accept that change.

Do anything we can to increase communication between us and the children we raise or teach. Stop at nothing. Even if they do not talk, we can talk, delivering the message that it does not have to be this way.

Make noise. Lots of noise. We must awaken our communities to the dangers of bullying, and that bullying is no longer child's play. Bullying is a killer and should be treated as such.

We must make it happen. We are the only ones who can.

"I watch the sun go down like any one of us
Hoping that the dawn will bring a sign
Of better days for those who will come after us
This time....."
– Ozzy Osbourne "Dreamer"

References

Adler, A. (1938). *Social Interest*. Boston, MA: Oneworld Publications

Allen, N. (CNN anchor). (2000, January 13). Michigan judge sentences Nathaniel Abraham to juvenile detention [Television broadcast]. Pontiac, MI: Cable News Network.

Alcoholics Anonymous, (1938). Akron: OH. Alcoholics Anonymous, Publisher.

American Psychiatric Association. (2000). *Diagnostic and Statistical Manual of Mental Disorders* (4th ed. text revision) Washington, DC: Author.

Champion, D. (2007). *The Juvenile Justice System: Delinquency, Processing and the Law*. Upper Saddle River, NJ: Pearson Education, Inc.

Coloroso, B. (2003). *The Bully, the Bullied, and the Bystander*. New York: NY: HarperCollins.

Emmons, N. (1986). *Manson in His Own Words*. New York, NY: Grove Press.

Hoover, J. & Oliver, R. (1996). *The Bullying Prevention Handbook*. Bloomington, ID: Solution Tree.

In the Mix. (n.d.). Retrieved April 15, 2007, from **http://www. inthemix.org**.

Kohut, M. (1985). *Charles Manson: How Society Created a Killer*. Unpublished master's thesis, University of Oklahoma, Norman: OK.

Kohut, M. (2000). United States Air Force Family Advocacy Program Clinician's Manual. Washington, DC: HQ AFMOA

McGrath, M. (2007). *School Bullying: Tools for Avoiding Harm and Liability*. Thousand Oaks, CA: Corwin Press.

McGraw, P. (1999). *Life Strategies: Doing What Works, Doing What Matters*. New York, NY: Hyperion.

Meloy, J. (Ed.). (1998). *The Psychology of Stalking*. San Diego, CA: Elsevier

Olweus, D. (1993). *Bullying at School*. Malden, MA: Blackwell.

Oncale v Sundowner (USSC 1998)

Randel, D. (2006). *Stopping School Violence*. Bloomington, IN: AuthorHouse.

Samaha, J. (2005). *Criminal Law*. Belmont, CA: Thompson Wadsworth.

Scaglione, J. & Scaglione, A. (2006). *Bullyproofing Children*. Lanham, MD: Rowman & Littlefield Education.

Vargas, Melissa. Bullying puts students in a dangerous position. (2006, December 4). *The Montana Standard*, p C1.

Varnava, G. (2002). *How to Stop Bullying in Your School.* London: David Fulton Publishers, Ltd.

Welty, E. (2007, May). *How to Stand Up to a Bully's Mom.* Redbook, 290. 88-90.

Remember

05.21.1998 — Springfield, Oregon

Kip Kinkel, 15, killed 2 students and wounded 22 others in the cafeteria at Thurston High School. Kinkel brought a gun to school the day before and was arrested. Later, authorities found his parents dead at his house.

Appendix

A Student's Anti-Bullying Pledge

We, the students of _____school, have decided to make our school free of bullying. We believe that all students have a right to an education, and to receive that education in a safe environment. We define bullying as pushing, kicking, hitting, destroying personal property, stalking, cyberbullying, gang intimidation or violence, name-calling, making fun of others' differences, excluding someone from our peer group, and laughing at others. We pledge to:

1. Treat others with respect and accept their differences in race, religion, intelligence, gender, national origin, or color.

2. Never be involved in bullying incidents or be a bully.

3. Never be a bystander in bullying incidents.

4. Report all incidents of bullying to a school staff member.

5. Follow our school's anti-bullying policy.

6. Help our teachers and school administrators develop an anti-bullying policy.

7. Provide emotional support for someone who has been bullied.

8. Participate in all school activities that support our no-bullying policy.

9. Be a good role model for others by being kind, respectful, and non-violent.

My signature and date: _____

A Teacher's Anti-Bullying Pledge

We, the faculty of _____school, agree to work with other staff members, students, and parents to stop bullying in our school. We believe that everyone has the right to receive an education in a safe environment. We define bullying as pushing, hitting, kicking, ridiculing, destroying property, laughing at others' race, religion, or gender, stalking, cyberbullying, gang intimidation, name-calling, excluding others, and violent behavior. We join our students in:

1. Developing a school anti-bullying policy. We will place the policy in every classroom, in the cafeteria, in the gym, and in the assembly hall.

2. Educating all students about bullying and its effects.

3. Supporting and encouraging a student who has been bullied.

4. Encouraging bystanders to report incidents of bullying immediately.

5. Offer counseling for bullies, victims, and bystanders.

6. Reporting all suspected bullying to the principal.

7. Working with the principal to devise a system of informing parents that their child is bullying others or has been a victim of bullying.

8. Fully enforcing disciplinary action against bullying.

9. Creating a school atmosphere where victims and bystanders feel safe in reporting incidents of bullying.

10. Developing anti-bullying practices through teaching children problem-solving skills, anger management, and social skills.

11. Displaying this document in my classroom so that all students know that I will not tolerate bullying.

Signature and date: _____

A Parent's Anti-Bullying Pledge

I, _____, am the parent of a child who attends _____ school. I will support the students, faculty, and other parents with children attending this school. I believe that all children have the right to receive an education in a safe environment. I understand bullying to be pushing, hitting, destruction of property, intimidating, threatening, gang activity, stalking, cyberbullying, name-calling, excluding others from peer groups, laughing at others, and making fun of others because of their race, color, national origin, religion, gender, and ridiculing. As a parent, I agree to:

1. Assist school faculty in developing and enforcing an anti-bullying policy for the school.

2. Never condone acts of bullying or bystanding by my own child(ren); bystanders are just as guilty as bullies.

3. Work with the school faculty and my children in educating them about respecting the rights of others, accepting differences among people, and showing kindness and tolerance of all adults and children.

4. Work with the school faculty to establish and enforce disciplinary action against bullies and bystanders.

5. Provide an atmosphere in my home that encourages reports by my child(ren) that they have been bullied or had observed bullying.

6. Teach my child(ren) to solve problems without violence,

anger management, communication skills, and social skills.

7. Participate in counseling with my child(ren) if they have been bullying, bystanding, or are victims of bullies.

Signature and date: _____

A Safety Checklist for Schools, Homes, and Communities

Zero-tolerance for bullying behavior can only be eliminated when schools, homes, and communities work together to establish a bully-free environment. This is a checklist for schools, homes and communities to measure their success in establishing an anti-bullying campaign designed to eliminate school bullying. This checklist is designed to precipitate discussions among school staff, parents, school board members, and legislatures. Each question can be answered "yes" or "no." "Maybe" answers indicate that the school et. al need to examine their anti-bullying policy to make certain it is in place, and is working effectively.

1. Does the school work closely with parents by providing information about the school's anti-bullying established policy?

2. Is there a zero-tolerance policy against violence, psychological or physical, in the school?

3. Does the school publicize its anti-bullying policy in the local newspaper, newsletters to parents, and other means?

4. Does the school make clear to families and community members that a no-violence policy is expected in these environments, as well as in the school?

5. Is the school clear and consistent in dealing with bullying and bystanding incidents, especially those that could be considered criminal acts?

6. Does the school take notice of violence in other schools to avoid the "copycat" syndrome in their own school?

7. Has the school principal and school board members publicly spoken to media personnel about their efforts to make the school bully-free?

8. Does the school promote a friendly, kind, atmosphere?

9. Has each student been informed about the school's anti-bullying policy?

10. Does the school promote personal responsibility for unkind actions towards other students?

11. Does the school have a policy against violent language and name-calling?

12. Does the school promote mediation between the bully and the victim to resolve the bullying incident or pattern in a conciliatory manner?

13. Are new students, staff, and school board members given information about the school's anti-bullying policy?

14. Are comprehensive records kept about each incident of bullying, e.g the bully, the victim, and the bystanders if known, for consistent monitoring?

15. Does the school provide staff hall monitors, cafeteria monitors, bathroom monitors, and monitors at school-sponsored activities?

16. Are groups like the Student Council actively involved in promoting anti-bullying policies?

17. Are both vulnerable and potentially violent students identified by the principal's or guidance counselor's office?

18. Is non-acceptance of bullying a prominent part of the curriculum for school classes?

19. Does the curriculum include lessons that foster self-esteem and respect for others?

20. Is media violence, and its effects, part of the school curriculum?

21. Is specific advice concerning personal safety a part of the curriculum?

22. Are problem-solving techniques that do not involve violence a part of the curriculum?

23. Are students taught what constitutes bullying and bystanding?

24. Are students taught how to be a good listener, how to be a reliable witness to incidents of bullying, how the law defines human rights, how to accept peers who are in some way different than other students, and the serious dangers of bullying?

25. Have the students, parents, and school staff all signed the pledge against toleration of bullying, and displayed those pledges in a prominent place?

Remember

12.07.1999 — Veghel, Netherlands

A 17-year-old student wounded one teacher and three students.

Author Biography

Margaret R. Kohut

Margaret Kohut is an Oklahoma native and still holds proudly to her "Midwestern drawl." She earned college degrees in English, Criminal Justice, and a Master's degree in Social Work. Her initial foray into human service work was as a correctional officer in both adult and juvenile maximum security correctional institutions. Margaret's unique job history includes being a courtroom bailiff and a fugitive recovery agent ("bounty hunter"), and she spent a year in the private practice of clinical social work specializing in adoption studies, pre-sentence investigations, probation and parole intervention, family therapy, and therapy with troubled juveniles. Margaret has a strong educational and vocational history of forensic counseling and addiction therapy.

Margaret served in the United States Air Force for seventeen years as a commissioned officer and clinical social worker providing psychotherapy services for active duty members, family members, and retirees. Margaret served the nation during Operation Desert Storm and Operation Iraqi Freedom. She is now a disabled veteran, conducting her full-time freelance writing business from her home. Margaret maintains national-level certifications in human services, as found in her CV. She is a prolific writer, having penned many award-winning publications for the Air Force on mental health issues, domestic violence, workplace violence, chemical dependency, trauma therapy, and adolescent acting-out behavior. As a civilian, Margaret co-authored an academic textbook on sexual serial killers and has been extensively published in the Canadian Journal of Adlerian Psychology and other academic publications. Margaret founded Rocky Mountain Way Freelance Writing in February 2006 after more than 20 years of non-commercial writing. Her lengthy CV attests to the success of her commercial writing abilities.

Margaret lives in Anaconda, Montana with her husband of 15 years, Lt. Col. (ret) Dr. Tristan Kohut, Medical Director of the Montana State Prison, and their 13 miniature Dachshunds; most of them are accomplished animal-assisted therapy dogs.

"Service to others is in my blood," Margaret says. "After the great honor of serving my country, I hope to help others through my writing and leave this world a better place than I found it."

Glossary

A

Accountability – Holding someone responsible for his or her actions

Aggression – Acting out, often in a violent manner, toward people and/or animals

Anti-bullying – A stance that is against bullying in all its forms

Anti-Bullying Act of 2005 (H.R. 284) – A bill that was introduced in the House of Representatives that includes cyberbullying in its definition of bullying behavior if the bullying is done of school computers and other forms of technology

Anti-Social Personality Disorder – A psychiatric condition in which the sufferer violates the rights of others or does not conform to socially acceptable behavior

Assault – A physical attack on another person

B

Blame – The act of holding another person or group responsible for your actions, faults, etc.

Bully – The tormenting of others by using verbal harassment, physical assault, or even other methods such as manipulation and gossip

Bully-proof – A term used to describe children who are immune to bullying, whether naturally or by instruction.

Bullycide – A suicide as the result of bullying.

Bystander – A person who observes but does not participate; bystanders may serve as enablers of bullies.

C

Civil Rights: Those rights established to all United States citizens through the thirteenth and fourteenth amendments. It is often used in reference to the rights that were extended to minority groups.

Common Concern Method – A method of working with bullies and victims that is designed to lessen the pathological impact of bullying on children and that helps bullies understand the feelings of their victims and helps all parties involved reach a solution.

Conduct Disorder – A mental health disorder that is often diagnosed in infancy, childhood, or adolescence that is characterized by a pattern of behavior in which the basic rights of others or societal norms are violated.

Cyberbullying – A form of bullying that is perpetrated on the Internet, especially via e-mail, instant messenger, and chat rooms.

D

Depression – A state of mental health characterized by extreme melancholy, sadness, and inadequacy.

Domestic violence – A form of physical, emotional, and verbal abuse directed towards one's significant other.

H

Harassment: To make repeated attacks against someone in an effort to disturb or hurt them.

Hate crime – A crime perpetrated against someone based on their race, gender, religion, sexual orientation, etc.

Hippo – An analogy used to help break down the denial of a problem and to help acknowledge that it needs to be addressed.

Hypervigilence – A state of heightened sensory sensitivity that allows one to detect threats.

I

In loco parentis – A legal concept in which educational personnel assume guardianship duties and responsibilities when children are at school.

Intervention – An attempt, whether by one person or a group, to stop a certain action; in this case, bullying.

Intimidation – A technique that combines threats and fear used to make a weaker person do something.

Isolation – Separation from a person or a group, especially socially.

J

Juvenile Justice System – The legal system in which juveniles are processed, adjudicated, and corrected.

M

Mean girls - A type of bullying perpetrated by girls in which backstabbing, exclusion, and rumors are used to isolate and terrorize a victim.

Mental Health: The condition of psychological stability.

Mobbing – The act of several bullies working together to harm their target.

N

Negligence – As related to bullying, the act of a school employee failing to act to prevent bullying and to protect victims, especially because they have a duty to do so.

O

Omerta – The rule of silence; often used in the mafia.

P

Peer group – A grouping of people based on their age.

Post-Traumatic Stress Syndrome - A condition characterized in which a person often relives traumatic events from his or her past.

R

Racial Slur: A disparaging remark made about someone's skin color.

Red flag – A term used to describe warning signs that a child is a bully or is the victim of bullying.

Rumor – Misinformation that is maliciously spread in order to isolate someone.

S

Self-esteem – A person's sense of self-worth and how much he or she values his or herself.

Sexual harassment – A form of harassment in which the victim is subjected to unwanted sexual comments and advances.

Stalking – The act of purposely and repeatedly following and harassing another person.

Substance abuse – The use of any addictive substance – be it drugs or alcohol – for non-therapeutic purposes.

Suicide – The act of taking one's own life.

Supreme Court: The highest court in the United States as established by Article III of the constitution. The rulings of the nine justices determine precedents for cases heard by lower courts.

T

Target – A person who is the aim of a bully, especially for ridiculing and exploitative purposes.

Tattletale – A person who reports others' wrongdoings to an authority figure.

Truancy – The failure of a child to attend school, especially an absence that is not legitimate.

U

Unconditional love – The act of loving someone regardless of his or her actions, beliefs, etc.

V

Victim – The person against whom a crime was committed; in this case, the target of a bully.

W

Witness – A person who sees an event take place.

Z

Zero tolerance – A policy that strictly enforces the rules and/or laws.

Index

A

Abuse 14, 15, 16, 20, 21, 39, 41,
   45, 47, 48, 49, 65, 66, 94,
   108, 109, 129, 143, 191,
   192, 195, 196, 217, 230

Accountability 41, 187, 220

Agenda 29, 63

Aggression 25, 41, 51, 59, 71,
   77, 78, 88, 163, 170, 193

Angry 52

Anti-bullying 29, 161, 167, 179,
   181, 183, 184, 188, 192,
   197, 198, 206, 207, 208,
   209, 213, 214, 216, 226,
   228, 230, 231, 234, 250,
   255

Anti-gay discrimination 216

Assault 11, 14, 36, 85, 87, 96,
   98, 103, 114, 128, 130, 139,
   174, 180, 216, 217, 222,
   223, 241, 243

Attorney 64, 85, 87, 97, 117, 122,
   204, 215, 222

B

Bad parents 59

Blame 51, 59, 60, 61, 64, 71,
   106, 148, 154, 165, 187,
   207

Bully-proof 83, 122, 135, 136,
   141, 142, 147, 149, 154,
   188, 205, 207

Bullycide 51, 67, 92, 98, 114,
   122, 207, 253, 254

Bystander 15, 37, 44, 45, 56, 58,
   63, 65, 81, 82, 83, 86, 87,
   115, 116, 117, 118, 146,
   147, 149, 150, 152, 156,
   192, 198, 199, 203, 209,
   244, 255

THE COMPLETE GUIDE TO UNDERSTANDING, CONTROLLING, & STOPPING BULLIES & BULLYING AT WORK:
A COMPLETE GUIDE FOR MANAGERS, SUPERVISORS, AND CO-WORKERS

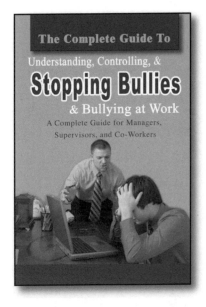

According to the Occupational Safety and Health Administration (OSHA), more than two million workers in the United States alone are victims of workplace violence each year, leading to millions of dollars lost in employee productivity. Many people believe that bullying occurs only among school-age children and fail to acknowledge the presence and devastation effects of bullying in the workplace.

In this new book, you will learn how to identify the problem of workplace bullying, how to define the workplace bully, how to identify characteristics of workplace bullies, how to bust bullying, and how to "bully-proof" your employees. This book discusses indicators of a toxic workplace, the causes of workplace bullying, and reasons why workplace bullying is perpetuated and unchallenged by other employees.

This book also provides solutions to end workplace violence. If you are a manager, a supervisor, or an employee and you suspect bullying is occurring, you need to read this book.

ISBN-10: 1-60138-236-7 • ISBN-13: 978-1-60138-236-8
288 Pages • Item # GSB-02 • $21.95

EMPLOYEE BODY LANGUAGE REVEALED: HOW TO PREDICT BEHAVIOR IN THE WORKPLACE BY READING AND UNDERSTANDING BODY LANGUAGE

Only 7 percent of communication is verbal and 38 percent is vocal. The largest chunk then, 55 percent, is visual. People form 90 percent of their opinion about you within the first 90 seconds of meeting you. Understanding body language is a skill that can enhance your life. This understanding can be a plus in the workplace. You can know what an employee or co-worker thinks and feels by examining their subconscious body language. And, like the world's best communicators, you can have strong body language that reflects confidence, competence, and charisma.

This groundbreaking new book will make you an expert on body language. You will have the ability to read people's minds. Would you like to know if a co-worker is interested or attracted to you, when an employee or co-worker is lying or telling the truth, how to make instant friends, and persuade and influence others? This book contains proven techniques that will make people, including employers and co-workers, like you and trust you. You can use your body language to your advantage by transmitting only the messages you want people to receive. This specialized book will demonstrate step by step how to use body language to your benefit in the workplace and in everyday situations.

ISBN-10: 1-60138-147-6 • ISBN-13: 978-1-60138-147-7
288 Pages • Item # EBL-01 • $21.95

To order call 1-800-814-1132 or visit www.atlantic-pub.com

How to Go to College on a Shoe String: The Insider's Guide to Grants, Scholarships, Cheap Books, Fellowships, and Other Financial Secrets

Costs of attending college are rising. With an 8 percent college inflation rate, the cost of college doubles every nine years. Currently, the average cost of attending a private four-year college is about $21,235 yearly, and the cost of attending a public university averages to $5,491 per year. These costs are just the beginning. When you add in the cost of books, room and board, and living expenses, the cost of attending a private college is $29,026, and the cost of attending a public university is $12,127 per year.

There is good news. More financial aid is available than ever before — over $134 billion.

In addition to scholarships and grants, this book will teach you hundreds of innovative ways to slash your college costs including: calculating your college budget, finding cheap textbooks, tax credits, tuition payment plans, federal funds, innovative dating ideas, medical & dental coverage, your car, your computer, spring break, and much more. Maybe saving money does not matter to you, perhaps you won the lottery. However, if you want to learn hundred of innovative ways to save thousands on your college costs, then this book is for you.

ISBN-10: 1-60138-020-8 • ISBN-13: 978-1-60138-020-3
288 Pages • Item # CGB-02 • $24.95

DID YOU BORROW THIS COPY?

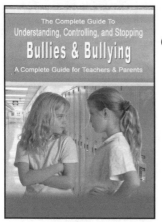

Have you been borrowing a copy of *The Complete Guide to Understanding, Controlling, and Stopping Bullies & Bullying: A Complete Guide for Teachers and Parents* from a friend, colleague, or library? Wouldn't you like your own copy for quick and easy reference? To order, photocopy the form below and send to:

Atlantic Publishing Company
1405 SW 6th Ave • Ocala, FL 34471-0640

YES!

Send me____copy(ies) of *The Complete Guide to Understanding, Controlling, and Stopping Bullies & Bullying: A Complete Guide for Teachers and Parents* (Item # CGB-02) for $24.95 plus $7.00 for shipping and handling.

Please Print

_____
Name

_____
Organization Name

_____
Address

_____
City, State, Zip

❏ My check or money order is enclosed. *Please make checks payable to Atlantic Publishing Company.*

❏ My purchase order is attached. *PO #* _____

www.atlantic-pub.com • e-mail: sales@atlantic-pub.com

Order toll-free 800-814-1132

FAX 352-622-1875

Atlantic Publishing Company
1405 SW 6th Ave • Ocala, FL 34471-0640

Add $7.00 for USPS shipping and handling. For Florida residents PLEASE add the appropriate sales tax for your county.

8. Murray the K: WINS New York 1964

   Courtesy of Peter Altschuler, Murray Kaufman's son, who invites Murray the K fans to visit www.tvclassics.com/mtk.htm.

9. Joey Reynolds: WKBW Buffalo, NY 1964, WXYZ Detroit 1966

   Courtesy of Joey Reynolds, WOR-AM, New York, with thanks to Jack Raymond, the award-winning DJ, for the aircheck.

10. Johnny Holliday: WINS New York March 1965

    Courtesy of Johnny Holliday of ABC Radio Sports, and the Johnny Holliday Collection on www.REELRADIO.com.

11. Don MacKinnon: KFWB Los Angeles 1965

    Courtesy of Doug MacKinnon, with thanks to Liz Salazar and Bobby Ocean for the aircheck.

12. Russ "The Moose" Syracuse: KYA San Francisco 1965-66, KFRC and KMPX-San Francisco

    Courtesy of Tracy Syracuse DePaola and the Syracuse family. Tapes from John Catchings (KFRC), Tom Gericke (KREB), and Russ Syracuse.

13. The Real Don Steele: KHJ Boss Angeles 1965

    Courtesy of Shaune Steele, who invites you to visit www.realdonsteele.com and to hear KRTH-FM's tribute to The Real Don Steele, produced by Keith Smith, at www.REELRADIO.com. Thanks to Tina DelGado.

14. Robert W. Morgan: KHJ Los Angeles 1966 and beyond

    Courtesy of Shelley Morgan and Susanna Morgan Enenstein. Thanks to REELRADIO.com, home of the Robert W. Morgan "Bossography" (produced by Kevin Gershan), and of the Michael Hagerty and Bob Green aircheck collections.

15. Bobby Ocean: KHJ Los Angeles 1975-1977, KFRC San Francisco 1983

    Thanks to Liz Salazar and Bobby Ocean (Bobby Ocean, Inc.), who's back on KFRC for the seventh time. Whatta guy!

16. Rick Dees: KIIS-FM Los Angeles

    Courtesy of Rick Dees of KIIS-FM and Premiere Radio Networks' "Rick Dees Weekly Top 40." Visit Rick at www.rick.com.

17. Scott Shannon: WMAK Nashville, mid-seventies, WHTZ (1983) and WPLJ New York

    Thanks to Scott Shannon of WPLJ-New York for his permission and airchecks.

Special thanks to Richard W. Irwin, president of REELRADIO, Inc., a non-profit organization dedicated to the preservation of classic Top 40 radio.

Producer: Ben Fong-Torres
Co-producer: Bobby Ocean
Executive Producer: Backbeat Books

NOTE: *This recording is intended for your private use. It may not be reproduced, distributed, broadcast, or sold.*
© *2001 Ben Fong-Torres and Backbeat Books.*

THIS JUST IN . . .

THE AUTHOR WISHES TO MAKE THE FOLLOWING CORRECTIONS AND NOTES:

My memories of childhood may be fuzzy, but that's still no excuse for saying that "How Much Is That Doggie in the Window?," the big early-fifties hit by Patti Page, was by Doris Day (Page 4). Sorry, Patti; sorry, Doris. I love you both.

Jerry Blavat, "The Geator with the Heater," was on WSSJ in Camden, New Jersey, not Philadelphia, as I said on Page 89. But that's a moot point now. He's currently heard on various New Jersey and Pennsylvania (but not Philly) stations along the "Geator Gold Radio" network. He's also on the Internet—which, I am happy to report, does include Philadelphia.

Scott Shannon's time in Nashville in the mid-seventies (Page 227) was at WMAK, not WMAQ, the Chicago radio landmark that switched call letters in August 2000.

On Page 103, several DJs are reported to have left their radio stations in the heat of the 1959 congressional investigation of payola. "Many of them would deny that it had anything to do with payola," I wrote. One of them, Robin Seymour, has stated that any changes in his employment at that time had no connection with the hearings in Washington, D.C. Seymour remains a successful broadcaster today.

Since the initial publication of this book in 1998, several personalities who were—and are—a major part of it have died. Robert W. Morgan, Frankie Crocker, Douglas "Jocko" Henderson, Bobby Dale, and Russ Syracuse will be remembered and loved as long as there are fans and airchecks. I was honored to write the script for the 1999 induction ceremonies of the Radio Hall of Fame, when Morgan was inducted.

THE HITS JUST KEEP ON COMING: THE AIRCHECKS

1. Welcome from Ben Fong-Torres
2. Alan Freed: WJW Cleveland 1954, WINS New York 1955
   Courtesy of Judith Fisher Freed and the Alan Freed Estate, who invite you to visit www.alanfreed.com.
3. Gary Owens: KEWB Oakland/San Francisco 1960 and 1959
   Courtesy of Gary Owens, whose radio show is heard on the nationally syndicated "Music of Your Life," and Pleasant Hillbilly CDs.
4. Casey Kasem: Buffalo, WBNY, 1960, KEWB 1962
   Casey Kasem hosts five programs from Premiere Radio Networks, including "American Top 40" with Casey Kasem. Thanks to Casey, Burns Media and Ron Lyons of KCBS-San Francisco for the airchecks.
5. Tom Donahue: KYA San Francisco 1961
   Courtesy of Raechel Donahue, whose radio and production credits include a documentary on FM radio for public television. Thanks to Steve Rood for the aircheck.
6. B. Mitchel Reed: WMCA New York 1963
   Courtesy of David Reed.
7. Dick Biondi: WLS Chicago 1963
   Courtesy of Dick Biondi of WJMK, Chicago, and the John Rook Collection on www.REELRADIO.com.